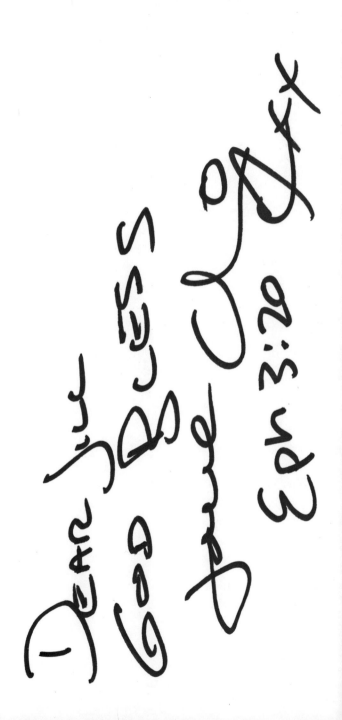

Dear Sue
God Bless
Jerome Clyde

Eph 3:20

A Life Unleashed

GIVING BIRTH
TO YOUR DREAMS

A Life Unleashed

GIVING BIRTH TO YOUR DREAMS

Christine Caine

Foreword by Joyce Meyer

NEW YORK   BOSTON   NASHVILLE

All Scripture quotations, unless otherwise indicated, are taken from *The Amplified Bible* (AMP).
The Amplified Bible, Old Testament. Copyright © 1965, 1987 by The Zondervan Corporation. *The Amplified New Testament,* copyright © 1954, 1958, 1987 by The Lockman Foundation. Used by permission.

Scripture quotations marked "NKJV" are taken from the New King James Version. Copyright © 1982 by Thomas Nelson, Inc. Used by permission. All rights reserved.

Scripture quotations marked "NIV" are taken from The Holy Bible, New International Version®. NIV®. Copyright © 1973, 1978, 1984 by International Bible Society. Used by permission of Zondervan Publishing House. All rights reserved.

Scripture quotations marked "NLT" are taken from the Holy Bible, New Living Translation, copyright © 1996. Used by permission of Tyndale House Publishers, Inc., Wheaton, Illinois 60189.

Warner Faith

Time Warner Book Group

1271 Avenue of the Americas, New York, NY 10020

Visit our Web site at www.twbookmark.com

Printed in the United States of America

First Warner Books printing: September 2004

10 9 8 7 6 5 4 3 2 1

Library of Congress Cataloging-in-Publication Data
Caine, Christine.
   A life unleashed : giving birth to your dreams / Christine Caine.
      p. cm.
   ISBN 0-446-57666-2
   1. Self-realization—Religious aspects—Christianity. I. Title.
   BV4598.2.C35 2004
   248.4—dc22   2004008287

This book is dedicated with all my love
to my beautiful daughter, Catherine Bobbie.

For You did form my inward parts; You did knit me together in my mother's womb.

I will confess and praise You for You are fearful and wonderful and for the awful wonder of my birth! Wonderful are Your works and that my inner self knows right well.

My frame was not hidden from You when I was being formed in secret [and] intricately and curiously wrought [as if embroidered with various colors] in the depths of the earth [a region of darkness and mystery].

Your eyes saw my unformed substance, and in Your book all the days [of my life] were written before ever they took shape, when as yet there was none of them.

(Psalm 139:13-16)

Contents

❧

Foreword

❧

Each one of us is a unique individual with a specific God-given destiny to fulfill. We each have dreams that only we can carry out. In order to do so, we must take the necessary steps to let go of what lies behind and take hold of what lies ahead.

The fact is that most of us have experienced some type of abuse, rejection, or hardship in our past. Although we cannot erase it, we can overcome it through a relationship with Jesus Christ. Second Corinthians 5:17 says, "If any person is [ingrafted] in Christ (the Messiah) he is a new creation (a new creature altogether); the old . . . has passed away. Behold, the fresh and new has come!"

I believe the foundation for finding freedom from our past

and making our dreams a reality is in understanding who we are in Christ. This knowledge is obtained through the continual study of God's Word. Jesus said, "If you abide in My word [hold fast to My teachings and live in accordance with them], you are truly my disciples. And you will know the Truth, and the Truth will set you free" (John 8:31-32).

I have learned that experiencing our full potential comes from living what the Word of God says instead of focusing on the disappointments and pain of our past. The facts about our past are powerless against the blood of Jesus and the Truth of His Word. What Satan meant for evil, God desires to use for our good and the good of others. I believe as we allow our thinking to be renewed by God's Word and cooperate with the leading of the Holy Spirit, we will begin to inherit His promised land for our lives.

Christine Caine is an awesome woman of God who loves the Lord and desires to see people set free from the bondage of their past and give birth to their God-given dreams. In *A Life Unleashed*, she shares her testimony of hope and healing, and explores how we can make our divinely inspired potential a reality. It is clear, practical, and easy to understand. It will challenge you to ask yourself some serious questions, and will help you take hold of the predestined purpose for your life—enabling you to experience the sweet satisfaction of walking in the perfect will of God.

Joyce Meyer
Joyce Meyer Ministries

A Quick Note

It's funny how God drops dreams and ideas into your heart at the most unlikely times and in the most interesting places. This book was conceived while I was standing in a bathroom the day I discovered I was pregnant with my first child.

At that point I had no real idea what *A Life Unleashed* would be, but I knew the nine months of my pregnancy would somehow form the fabric of it. As the baby inside me grew and developed, so did this book. I discovered that conceiving, carrying, and giving birth in the natural has much in common with actualizing our potential and realizing our dreams.

When I found out I was pregnant I didn't know what the

process would entail. My knowledge of babies was limited. All I knew was it started with conception and finished with me holding a baby (morning sickness, an overactive bladder, and maternity clothes were somewhere in between). Similarly, when we commit to fulfilling our potential we begin a journey that will ultimately take us to the delivery room and help us birth our dreams.

Overall the pregnancy experience was a joyful one for me. I particularly liked it when people told me I had to eat more now that I was eating for two. I also appreciated how nice people were to me. They always gave up their seat for the woman with the oversized belly bounding toward them. And I liked the fact that for nine months the only things I had to pick up were a knife and fork! Of course there were a few aspects of my pregnancy I would rather forget—like the nausea, not being able to drink coffee or eat chocolate, and of course contractions!

Regardless, I pressed through the discomfort (I really didn't have much choice) knowing on the other side my dream of having a baby would be realized. The moment I held my little girl, I knew all the stretching, adjustments, sacrifices (yes, even saying goodbye to Starbucks), and labor pains were worth it.

I've learned that life is like this. Although we face challenges and obstacles along the way, we can still give birth to our dreams. My life is a testimony to this fact. God has loved, forgiven, healed, freed, and restored me, and now I'm living the life of my dreams.

You may have thought you were picking up a book of quirky pregnancy stories. It is that—but it's so much more. I've laid it all on the line for you, revealing intimate details about my journey so far, and how I've overcome to have all God has for me.

To help you get the most out of *A Life Unleashed*, it has been designed in nine sections, one for each month of pregnancy. Each section ends with a "Walk It Out," which offers practical tips and guidelines designed to help you implement the thoughts and principles of this book in your own journey to fulfilling your God-given destiny.

My hope is that *A Life Unleashed* will stir you, challenge you, make you laugh, and perhaps even make you cry. But most of all I trust it will inspire you to allow God to unlock your dormant dreams and give you the courage to pursue them.

Now that your curiosity is piqued, grab a coffee (my preferred choice is a skinny latte), find a quiet spot (even if it's the bathroom), and brace yourself!

Love,
Chris

Section 1

CONCEIVE

✺ Diary Entry

I'm so excited to be on vacation in Australia's beautiful Whitsunday islands. Nick and I were overdue for a relaxing, fun vacation, and this promises to be a week of just that (if the nausea doesn't get in the way). It's now three days into the trip, and I am feeling worse by the minute. I've been feeling queasy and sleepy for ten days. Even lying on the beach soaking up the sun seems too much like hard work.

As I pulled on my swimsuit earlier today I jokingly said to Nick, "Maybe I'm pregnant!" Nick's only response was an expression of utter disbelief. Neither of us really thought pregnancy was even a remote possibility since we just started trying. Besides Nick and I spend a lot of time on different sides of the globe, which is generally not conducive to making babies!

As unlikely as pregnancy was I still thought a trip to the pharmacy was warranted, even if just for the practice. Nick agreed to come with me . . . reluctantly I'm sure, as he would have much preferred being out on a Jet Ski.

At the pharmacy we were greeted by a wall of pregnancy tests. Instinctively Nick moved toward the men's grooming section, leaving me with the job of choosing the right one. This was definitely uncharted territory. What criteria do you use to select a pregnancy test? Shape, size, the shade of blue? I did what any reasonable person would do—I chose the one with the nicest packaging. As I read the back of the kit I realized the process was pretty technical and there was a relative margin for error (this had a lot more to do with me than the test), so I picked up a spare one just in case.

Back at our hotel room with bladder at the ready (I hadn't been to the bathroom for hours) and test in hand, I made a beeline for the bathroom. I skimmed over the test instructions; I knew clear meant no baby and a blue line was a good indication the nine months ahead of us would be very different from the nine months just passed.

I broke open the packaging and got so confused I had to call Nick in to explain the process to me. After a few pointers I was ready to give it a go. However a slight miscalculation and bad aim (my hand-eye coordination has always been a little off) caused me to pee on my hand and down my leg, rendering the test completely unusable. Nick couldn't believe that, while man has developed computer technology that connects the world and unlocks the secrets of DNA, I could not get a simple home pregnancy test right.

Thank goodness I had anticipated the unpredictability of the female point-and-shoot and had had enough foresight to buy a spare. Though unsuccessful, the trial run had buoyed my confidence. I now knew that concentration and meticulous aim would bring success. Hooray, I hit the target! Now for the wait.

Only there was no wait! In about 0.0009 seconds a thin blue line appeared in the second window. I fumbled for the instructions. There it was: if both windows were blue, it was 99.9% certain I was pregnant.

Stunned, I stood staring at the thin blue line not saying a word. Nick, too, stared at the small tube dumbfounded, trying to comprehend what this little blue line really meant. A wave of incredible elation came over both of us, as did that feeling you get when you realize something just happened that will change your life forever.

We're having a baby!

(Note to self: wash test and keep to show all the baby's friends at his/her twenty-first birthday party)

It's Supernatural

It all started with a thin blue line. This wasn't just any old line—lines don't usually cause perfectly sane people to jump up and down, squealing in excitement. No, this line signified we had hit the baby jackpot! After six years of marriage Nick and I (and my Greek mother) knew it was time to bring a baby Caine into the world. We had prayed, we had planned, and now we had conceived.

As I stood in the bathroom that day staring at the thin blue line, it gradually sank in that the line represented more than just proof I could successfully take a pregnancy test (minor miracle)—more incredibly, it demonstrated I was now carrying in me a life in seed form. Eventually this small seed would become a baby, then a toddler, then an adolescent, and in time, an adult. The baby would walk, talk, think, dream, learn to read and write, relate to others, and do great things for God. It was hard to imagine all this would come from something that at this point could only be seen through a microscope.

I began reading every book on childbirth I could find. The things I discovered made it even more apparent that

nothing about my pregnancy was accidental (although it happened a little faster than we'd expected). Did you know, for example, there are only thirty days in a year when a woman is
likely to conceive? Or that the egg has only twenty-four hours
to be fertilized before it dies, and within one hour of ejacula-
tion ninety-nine percent of all the sperm die? What are the
odds! The more I learned about conception and childbirth,
the more I realized it's a miracle any woman ever gets pregnant!
Contrary to what some of us were taught in school, our conception wasn't the result of a biological game of Russian
roulette. The evidence all points to some amazing craftsman-
ship on God's part. This brought to mind, and further con-
firmed, something that first became obvious to me years earlier
when my father passed away—that each of us exists not by
accident, but by design and for a purpose.

When I was nineteen, I cradled in my arms the lifeless
body of my father—a victim of cancer. I realized at that very
moment that something was missing. Although I could still
see my dad, touch him, and smell him, his intellect and spirit
had disappeared. Surely his life had to have meaning. It had to
be part of a bigger picture, a greater plan. For his life to have
been limited to a brief, meaningless existence made no sense to
me. As I reeled from the fresh realization I would never see my
dad on earth again, I began to search for the intangible *something* that would explain the why of our existence.

This experience altered my life forever. From that moment

on I knew there had to be more to life than being conceived by accident, living without purpose, and dying without hope. It was clear to me life is much more than a random cosmic coincidence. God created us intentionally and with a purpose.

> For we are God's [own] handiwork (His workmanship), recreated in Christ Jesus, [born anew] that we may do those good works which God predestined (planned beforehand) for us [taking paths which He prepared ahead of time] that we should walk in them [living the good life which He prearranged and made ready for us to live]. *(Ephesians 2:10)*

As much as Nick would love to credit our conceiving so quickly to his gene pool (he's the youngest of thirteen children), conception begins in the mind of God. We all existed in eternity long before our parents came into the equation. The great news is that before time began God created each one of us for a purpose and gave us the ability to fulfill that purpose.

It Always Starts Small

When our baby was conceived, Nick's DNA combined with mine to create a unique genetic blueprint that would never again be repeated. In all of history—past, present, and future—there would be no one quite like our little baby! Nick and I just hoped the baby would have my feet and his chin.

Despite the fact the embryo in my womb was smaller than a grain of rice and looked more like a fish than a human being, the baby's entire genetic code was already determined—gender, hair color, eye color, height, and personality. How it all fit in there I'll never understand.

At conception the result of the collision between sperm and egg didn't seem like a big deal. But from this small beginning would come a baby. However it would be nine exciting (sometimes excruciating) months of development before that potential was fully realized.

Many of us view ourselves as tiny embryos. We feel small and think we have little to offer the world. Regardless of how we think and feel, God didn't design us to stay small. He created us full of incredible potential that is yet to be unleashed.

Potential is the difference between what is *actual* and what is *possible*—the unexposed ability, reserved strength, unused success, dormant gifts, hidden talents, and latent power that lies within each one of us. Potential is:

- The person we're still to become.
- Where we can go but still haven't been.

- All we can do but haven't yet done.
- Where we can reach but haven't yet aimed.

All of creation (yes, including you) possesses the hidden ability to be greater than what it is today. In us right now are the seeds to be all God has destined us to be. Only He can take us from where we are to the life He has called us to live.

As our designer He knows better than anyone our innate capabilities. His desire is that we birth the dreams and ideas He implanted in us. Like all good designers God provided us with a manual, the Bible, to help us on the journey of actualizing our potential. When we apply God's Word to our lives, we discover we can be so much more than we currently are. Building our lives on the Word promises to bring great success.

> Do not let this Book of the Law depart from your mouth; meditate on it day and night, so that you may be careful to do everything written in it. Then you will be prosperous and successful. *(Joshua 1:8 NIV)*

If you commit yourself to living according to His Word your potential will be unlocked, and in time, what may look small now will grow into something significant. Whatever you may think about yourself, and whatever your life has looked like up to this point, know this—God created you for so much more. Don't underestimate God's Truth! The life and dreams God has placed in you—the seeds of greatness—will be unleashed.

ᔕ

Conceive

Thinking about what it took to conceive . . . my purpose and dreams, I realize now it wasn't something that hit me like a thunderbolt or miraculously fell out of the sky knocking me out cold. It required that I get to know the Creator of the Universe (not a bad job title!) in a real and meaningful way. This is the key to unlocking our dreams. So from the laboratory of my life, here are some practical hints on how to discover the dreams, desires and purpose God has for you.

1. Ask God on a Date

Far from being sacrilegious, God wants to date us! He wants to spend time with you and He wants you to get to know Him better. He knows that conceiving a dream will take a head-on collision between you and Him. So, where do you take God for a date? (Having made the world, finding somewhere new is difficult.) Why not try:

- Going for a walk with God before burying yourself in the kitchen in the morning for lunch-making duty.
- Chatting with God as you drive to work (completely ignore the people staring from the car next to you), rather than listening to the stereo.
- Taking God on a shopping trip. He is very honest about how big your thighs look in those pants.
- Inviting God out for coffee—He is well-known for leaving his coffee untouched, which means you always get a second cup!

2. Ask God the BIG Questions

God knows about your cellulite, and the twenty-seven creams you've tried to get rid of it! He knows everything about you. As your relationship with God moves from casual dating to a daily commitment, it's essential you put the blemish concealer away and allow God to stir up all that's in your heart. You might start with asking Him:

- To ignite your passion.
- To reveal areas in your life that might need some work. Maybe it's some of your reactions, responses, or relationships.
- To help you let go of anything that will stop you living the life He has for you.

➤ Who is going to win this year's Super Bowl. (What do you have to lose?)

3. Ask God to Move In

When a newly married couple moves into their first home, they have no real clue what life is going to look like, but they embark on the adventure together regardless. This is exactly what it's like when we ask God to move into our lives permanently. If we're willing to do what it takes to make this partnership work (even when it's painful!) we will see all our dreams realized.

➤ Be open to change—Get used to doing things God's way.
➤ Be willing to compromise—Obedience is less painful than regret.
➤ Be willing to accept—the things you cannot change (even smelly socks).

Section 2

BELIEVE

❂ Diary Entry

I'm officially a baby incubator, or not so officially because so few people know I'm pregnant. I have to say I'm a little freaked out by it all. Not because I'm pregnant (yippee!), but because I have absolutely no clue about what lies ahead in this whole pregnancy adventure. I know nothing about babies. I'm not my mom! I don't even know how to put a diaper on! I've hardly even held a baby before. It's all so surreal!

(Take a big breath, Christine)

To put my mind at ease, I, the queen of lists, have made a list of everything that needs doing before the baby arrives in March. I started the list while reliving last night's Thai curry (note to self: stay away from red chili paste) in the office bath-room (wave after nauseous wave).

After consulting my pregnancy manual, the list has come to-gether quite nicely. Well at least it's a good starting point. I may have to rework it two or three times during the coming months to make sure I haven't overlooked anything important.

Baby List—Draft 1

1. Find obstetrician.
2. Squeeze in checkup.
3. Remind myself to keep baby a secret for at least twelve weeks (this is killing me!).
4. Book hospital.
5. Buy crib.
6. Buy baby clothes.
7. Buy really cute onesies and little baby socks.
8. Buy a baby changing table.
9. Read *Supernatural Childbirth*.
10. Decide whether we're going to move.
11. If yes, find a new house.
12. Paint baby room (Nick).
13. Remember to be in town for all key checkups.
14. Buy diapers.
15. Buy baby bath.
16. Buy baby bottles and sterilizer.

17. Buy breast pads.
18. Buy stroller.
19. Buy pacifiers.
20. Buy baby bag.
21. Exercise.
22. Do hospital tour.
23. Sign up for childbirth classes.
24. Buy maternity clothes (very frightening).
25. Schedule maternity leave.
26. Choose name(s).
27. Decide on nanny.
28. Have baby shower.
29. Send out baby shower thank-you notes.
30. Make e-mail and phone list for announcing baby's birth.
31. Prepare bag for hospital (note to self: buy new pajamas).
32. Remember to take hospital bag (Nick).
33. Have film for cameras (Nick).
34. Remember to take cameras (Nick).
35. Have baby.
36. Announce birth to all the world.
37. Lie in hospital bed recovering.

I showed Nick the list. He was not as excited about it as I was, particularly the fact that so many of the entries started with the word buy. *I explained that the list was as much for his benefit as my own. To this he nodded approvingly and told me that if it helped me stay sane it would be to everybody's benefit! (Ha-ha Nick.)*

God's in Control

After reveling in the fact we had conceived and were going to have a baby, Nick and I had to make some serious mental adjustments. Our life was never going to be the same again. We were very aware that having the biological capability to conceive and actually being parents were two very different things. We had a lot to learn!

At this time I was traveling and preaching two weeks of every month, speaking to churches, leaders, women, and young people (let me tell you . . . morning sickness and jet lag don't mix!), while Nick ran a successful business back home. Baby plans had caused us to reevaluate our life and make some significant decisions about the next stage. These included where we were going to live, how our ministry would look with a baby in the equation, and of course, what color we were going to paint the baby's room.

Our dream was for the opportunity and financial provision that would allow Nick, the baby, a nanny, and me to travel together ministering around the world. This was as likely as the Red Sea parting, but I had faith that if it happened once it could happen again! Nick and I were having enough trouble assembling the crib, let alone trying to work out how to make our dream a reality. We knew both would take a miracle. To facilitate the realization of our dream we had to trust that God was in control of our rapidly changing life, and that He would make a way for our dream to come true.

Believing we would make it through this next season was essential, but believing isn't always easy. It takes faith to believe you're actually capable of being all God says you can be. It takes faith to trust He is in complete control particularly when all the evidence is to the contrary. However daunting our circumstances or situation may appear—God is bigger.

I didn't realize just how important this revelation was until a few years ago, one week before my thirty-third birthday. I had just finished one appointment and had ten minutes to swallow some lunch before the next. As I sat down to have the first bite of my favorite beef vindaloo my cell phone rang. I wanted to ignore it but being a product of the twenty-first century I had to answer.

I was greeted by a very distraught sister-in-law who, after making sure I could talk, thrust the phone into the hands of George, my thirty-five-year-old brother. A common characteristic of Greeks is high emotion and high voice pitch, but what I heard from the other end of the phone was unusual even for my brother. Sobbing, George told me he had just received a letter from the Department of Community Services notifying him he had been adopted at birth. That morning he had dropped by my mom's place while she was out. As he arrived he intercepted the postman who was carrying the ill-fated letter. If it had been five minutes later or any other day he wouldn't have been there and never would have received the mail.

Thinking this was all a big mistake I joked about how this explained why he was a six-foot giant and I was a five-foot nothing! I told him to call Community Services and explain they had made a huge administrative error and sent the letter to the wrong person.

I was fully expecting George to call me right back laughing about how mistakes like that could really shake a person up. Instead, when the call came George was hysterical.

"Christine, it's true. They told me my biological mother was a fifteen-year-old girl who had become pregnant. They told me where I went to school, when I was immunized, and when I got married. They have my entire life on file!"

In that instant, I immediately thought of my mom who was about to unwittingly walk into a very volatile situation. I begged my brother not to mention the letter to Mom until I arrived at the house. I hung up and phoned Nick. I filled him in on the crisis and asked him to meet me at Mom's place.

I pulled up in front of the house only to see that Mom

had already arrived. I sprinted inside just in time to witness George handing her the letter. The look in Mom's eyes was enough to confirm the truth: George was adopted.

As emotions started to flare I, the mediator, tried to calm everybody down. George wanted to know everything. Why had my parents kept it a secret? Who were his real parents? Why didn't they want him?

Eventually everyone settled down enough to gather around the table and hear the facts. Tears poured down Mom's face as she told us that although there was no bio-logical reason she could not conceive, after several years of trying to get pregnant without success she and my dad had decided to adopt.

She explained that they chose to never tell George about being adopted because they considered him to be their own. Their intention was never to deceive or hurt him. There had just never seemed to be a right time to share the truth. Nor had they expected adoption laws to change so dramatically in thirty-five years. They never thought he'd find out.

We all sat around the dinner table, the same table around which we had shared many family meals, as Mom told us the story and tried to answer all our questions. The anger, confusion, and tears were eventually replaced by relative calm. Although stunned by Mom's disclosure, I was glad it was all out in the open. Now we could deal with this as a family and move on with our lives.

Then came a deathly silence. My mom lifted her head and looked at me from across the table. My eyes met hers. I knew there was something she wasn't telling me.

"Christine, since we're telling the truth, do you want to know the whole truth?" I braced myself for the worst and felt the blood drain from my face.

"I've been adopted too?" I asked uncertainly. She nodded in confirmation.

My very next comment astounded even me.

"Am I still Greek?" I blurted. (What can I say? I needed to be sure all those years of being taunted for being an ethnic minority were not in vain!). She nodded again.

I was completely numb and totally confused. Everything my mom had just explained to George also applied to me.

After an hour or so of my own questions there was nothing left to say. I hugged Mom and told her I loved her. I explained to Nick that I needed to process this bombshell on my own and that I would meet him at home later that night.

I left Mom's house and got into my car. I was crying so much it was a wonder I got the car started at all. As I drove, the magnitude of my mom's disclosure sank in. Everything I believed about who I was—my name, where I was born, and who my parents were—was untrue. I didn't know anything about the circumstances surrounding my conception—whether I was a result of an adulterous affair, rape, or a one-night stand. As I tried to process this new reality, I re-called the words of Psalm 139:

> For You did form my inward parts; You did knit me to-gether in my mother's womb. I will confess and praise You for You are fearful and wonderful and for the awful won-der of my birth! Wonderful are Your works, and that my inner self knows right well. My frame was not hidden from You when I was being formed in secret [and] intricately and curiously wrought [as if embroidered with various col-ors] in the depths of the earth [a region of darkness and mystery]. Your eyes saw my unformed substance, and in Your book all the days [of my life] were written before ever they took shape, when as yet there was none of them. *(Psalm 139:13-16)*

I had heard this Scripture hundreds of times. I had even preached it myself on many occasions. But it was only at that point that the Word came alive to me. I realized that al-though I may not have known the facts surrounding my conception and birth, I knew the Truth of God's Word. He knew me from before time began, and He intentionally cre-ated me. No facts can alter that Truth. It was this revelation that would be the catalyst for me coming to terms with my adoption.

God Values Every Seed

Although I was shocked to find out I was adopted, God knew it all along because He knows everything (yep, even your natural hair color).

Life sometimes serves up a surprise. It may be the loss of a job, a divorce, financial difficulties, sickness, or the death of a loved one (or even the discovery you're adopted). Whatever it is, we need to understand that, even though it may have shocked, disillusioned, or disappointed us, God is not caught off guard. He knew about it all along. He has equipped us to make it through these storms and He promises to sustain us in the midst of our trials. He is right there with us spurring us on so we'll become all He says we can be.

If we allow the challenges and obstacles to overwhelm us, we can lose hope and abort the very dreams God has placed in us. *Abortion* can be defined as premature termination resulting in destruction. Basically it's the destruction of potential before it has a chance to be realized. Whether the abortion of a fetus or the abortion of spiritual seed, it is the ultimate tragedy because it robs life of its essence and denies the future the value contained within that life.

At one of my earliest prenatal checkups my doctor asked me a very sobering question. "Do you want to have an amniocentesis?" This is a test recommended for pregnant women aged thirty and over (I was thirty-five) because women of that age are at a statistically higher risk of developing complications during pregnancy. The procedure itself is potentially dangerous because the uterus must be pierced to draw out amniotic fluid for testing.

My response to the doctor was rhetorical, "What for?" (And it wasn't because I was petrified of needles . . . although this thought had crossed my mind.)

Taking my question literally the doctor began to explain that the test would determine if my baby had any deformities (just hearing that word cut to my heart). If abnormalities were indicated I could then choose to terminate the pregnancy.

I was overwhelmed by what I heard although I knew the doctor was just doing her job. My response was absolute.

"Even if some test found that my baby had a disability, I would not need to hear any options." I explained to her that when it comes to the issue of life and death I have no authority. Only God can give life and only He has the right to take it away. My explanation was met with a profound silence. Needless to say I didn't take the test. Nick and I knew that regardless of our baby's mental and physical condition there was great potential in that seed, and we were committed to seeing it realized.

The conversation with my doctor caused me to think

about my biological mother and the choice she had to make thirty-five years earlier. I knew she was twenty-three, Greek, unmarried, and pregnant in a culture that would completely ostracize her for such a thing. She also lived in a time when there was little social support for unmarried mothers. The prevailing practice at that time was to strongly encourage single mothers to offer their babies up for adoption rather than keep them.

I cannot comprehend what it must have been like for her. She must have had incredible courage to give birth to me under such circumstances. I'm sure my mother endured loneliness, heartache, anguish, and despair—not to mention thirty-two hours of labor—to bring me into the world. I'll forever be thankful to this incredible woman who, although she had not planned to have me, carried me to term and gave me up for adoption instead of aborting me. Without the price my biological mother paid, all the innate potential contained within my unborn seed would have died with me, never to be realized.

Imagine if she had made a different choice. No me! No wife for Nick and no mom for my baby. (There would also be no book for you to read, no anecdotes to humor you . . . the list goes on.) My biological mother's decision also gave my mom the opportunity to know what it was like to hold a newborn baby, to give me a name, to dress me in frilly outfits (only to see them torn and dirtied as I slid on the floor or rolled in the grass), and to see me grow into all God created me to be.

Just as my mother had to pay a big price to have me, there is also a price we must be willing to pay to see our dreams become reality. Unfortunately, too often things like fear, past experiences, current circumstances, disappointments, rejection, criticism, hurt, insecurities, offences, unforgiveness, and ignorance cause us to give up and abort our dreams.

Perhaps it was a dream to start a business that was squashed by the fifteenth bank manager to reject your business proposal; or a university degree put on hold indefinitely after being told that school is no place for a single mother; or a childhood dream of being an actress or singer derailed after another audition door was slammed in your face. Or it may just be you don't believe you're good enough, talented enough, or worthy enough to achieve anything more than you already have. A teacher may have said you were stupid and would never amount to anything. A parent may have told you they wished you were never born. A friend may have rejected you or made you feel insignificant and small.

If we allow them, these things can take us off course and cause us to give up on our dreams. I've actually met many people who've done exactly this; I was able to identify them because I was once one of them! Often they are plagued by what I call Potent Potential-Destroyers (or PPDs). So deadly are these PPDs that if they could be bottled, UN weapons inspectors would be searching for them. They can take us away from our destiny and thwart our future.

The great news is that if we choose to overcome these PPDs and other obstacles that may come our way, we will give birth to our dreams.

Potent Potential-Destroyers

Many different things can destroy our potential but most of them can usually be traced to the following six Potent Potential-Destroyers.

Potent Potential-Destroyer 1: A Lack of Faith

One of the biggest threats to our potential is a lack of faith. I remember the day I foolishly agreed to jump off a bridge, albeit with an oversized rubber band around my ankles. As I stood on the edge of a rather deep precipice, eyes clamped shut, I had to put a lot of faith in that piece of elastic—not to mention faith in the man who fastened it to my legs.

I froze in launch position for what felt like forever. I was gripped by fear—what if the elastic broke? Hitting the ground at an extreme speed wasn't the way I envisioned myself dying!

As I hesitated I recalled the time I jumped off the roof of my house at age seven thinking I was Superman, only to realize I wasn't. Not willing to make the same mistake twice I began to step away from the edge. I could feel everyone's eyes on me as I walked away. I imagined what they all thought about my inability to take the plunge. I didn't really care as long as I was still standing on solid ground!

It was fear that paralyzed me into inaction on the bridge that day. And fear can cause us to walk away from our dreams. Fear is the opposite of faith and is the deadliest enemy to our potential. We all have fears. Some came from our childhood (like sleeping with your light on because you were scared of the boogeyman) and others have come from bad experiences (the big spider that somehow got inside your car and scurried up your arm while you were driving). Regardless of the origin of our fears we must have the courage to confront them or they will cripple us.

If you're serious about seeing your dreams fulfilled, I guarantee there'll come a point where you have to choose between faith and fear. Do you jump into the unknown or stay safe in the comfortable? Although taking the leap may seem risky, even crazy, it's faith that will take us to our dreams. I love what Joyce Meyer says—"Do it afraid."[i] Faith will equip us to do what we've never done before—usually what most others are too afraid to do—and achieve what we never thought possible. The key is choosing to jump into the faith adventure!

Potent Potential-Destroyer 2: Indecision

Another PPD is indecision. This one has gotten the best of me on a few occasions. One of the most vivid and devastating times was the night of my eighteenth birthday. It was the first time my parents had let me go to the local Greek dance with my cousins. I had waited in anticipation for this night for so long. Time and again I imagined myself walking into the room wearing one of my taffeta numbers (oh, how I loved the puffy sleeves!). As I made my grand entrance everyone would turn to stare at me, and all the boys would think I was so cute they'd be willing to line up for hours to dance with me! (See the movie *My Big Fat Greek Wedding* for more details.)

The big day finally arrived. I wanted to look perfect so by early afternoon I locked myself in my room, turned my stereo up, and began the preening process. Everything was going well until I opened my closet door. I couldn't decide what to wear. I proceeded to try on everything I owned. I tried short skirts, long skirts, long pants, short sleeves, long sleeves, no sleeves, high heels, and no heels. I was literally buried in the valley of indecision by the contents of my wardrobe!

Finally I emerged, a vision of loveliness (the blue eye shadow really complemented the outfit) only to be told that my ride got so sick of waiting they left without me. They had tried knocking but the music was so loud I didn't hear them. My indecision caused me to miss what at that point would have been the best night of my life!

The lesson we can all learn from my traumatic experience is that indecision can cause us to miss our dreams. Sometimes we choose to sit on the fence and procrastinate for so long the opportunity sails right by us. We may even try to spiritualize our indecision by convincing ourselves we haven't heard from God. Yes, we need to ask for the Holy Spirit's leading, but I believe there are some decisions God is waiting for us to make before He opens or closes a door.

I dare you . . . the next time you're in a restaurant pick something from the menu before asking everyone else what they're having, and stick with your choice. Seize the day! Make a decision and surprise yourself!

Potent Potential-Destroyer 3:
A Lack of Vision

Nick and I spend a great deal of time sleeping in hotel rooms because of all the traveling we do. It can really create havoc at nighttime, particularly when you're attempting to get to the bathroom with the least disruption possible. The lack of vision hampers my navigational skills (further exacerbated by the fact I don't want to open my eyes) and my sense of direction goes right out the window. On a few occasions, my sleepy body has nearly gone out the window (an all too literal demonstration of Proverbs 29:18, "Where there is no vision . . . the people perish").

Similarly a lack of vision for our life causes us to wander aimlessly, living without purpose and constantly bumping into walls and stumbling over obstacles. Our ability to see our future as a current reality is one of the greatest keys to realizing our dreams. Vision is the fuel that keeps us passionately pursuing our dreams even when they seem a long way off.

The enemy will consistently try to blur or limit our vision because he knows without clear vision we will never live the life God destined us to live. (This is such a key PPD I've dedicated an entire section of the book to it, so keep reading.)

Potent Potential-Destroyer 4:
A Lack of Wisdom

Do you know what it feels like to be horribly lost? I don't mean the time when you hid in the toy aisle only to realize your mom was already at the checkout. I'm talking big-dark-forest kind of lost.

A few years ago, some friends and I were on vacation in the far north of Australia. One day we decided to go four-wheel driving in the Daintree Rainforest. Being the Girl Scout that I am (literary license in use here) I thought I could navigate our way through the forest without a map. It was only later that I discovered the track we were on was one of Australia's foremost off-road routes, and there we were totally inexperienced and in the middle of the rain season.

The hours that followed were like the plot of a bad movie. First we got the rental car stuck in the mud so we were forced to find our way out by foot. This included crossing a crocodile-infested river (thankfully we were ignorant of this fact when we made the crossing). Then the rain began to pour. We had no food, no flashlight, no shelter, and no idea where we were. I was certain we were all going to die because we hadn't told anyone our plans. It could have been days before anyone noticed we were gone.

Exhausted, we decided to stop for the night. As we huddled together to try to keep warm, one of my friends decided he would continue to walk on in an attempt to sound the alarm. Those of us that were left were scared beyond words. We tried to stay optimistic but with every hour that passed we were less convinced we'd be found alive. It was the longest night of my life.

Just when I thought we were doomed I heard the sweetest sound I'd ever heard. A helicopter was hovering above us; hanging out of the door was my friend waving excitedly. We were saved! In our case a lack of wisdom—or as I like to call it, stupidity—almost cost us our lives (death is the ultimate potential-destroyer).

A lack of wisdom can compromise our destiny. I believe this is the reason God spends so much time in Proverbs reiterating how important it is to seek wisdom. He knows wisdom will bring knowledge and understanding that will help us live the life He has for us. I encourage you to never leave behind your map and your guide—the Word of God and the Holy Spirit—as you journey through life.

Potent Potential-Destroyer 5:
A Lack of Commitment

My Greek uncle often laments the fact that people's levels of commitment is waning. He reminisces about the days when a handshake was as good as a signed contract, when you could secure the purchase of twelve cows on the strength of your word.

It's a sad fact that people aren't as committed to each other as they once were, be it in marriage, business, friendships, or in church life. What's equally sad is that many people find it difficult to stay committed to themselves and their dreams.

It takes unwavering stickability to birth our dreams when distractions, opportunities, or even good offers come to divert our focus. Every extraordinary achievement is the result of a daily commitment to our dreams and the process that will make them a reality. (This too is so vital I have committed a whole section to it.)

Potent Potential-Destroyer 6:
Seeing Obstacles Not Opportunities

In junior high my dream was to be the high jump champion of my school. I would have come close if the bar had stopped getting in the way. I spent more time walking under the bar than going over it! With every failed attempt my high jumping dream seemed to be slipping further and further away.

My perspective was radically turned around the night of my school dance. A dance is not a dance without a limbo competition. The music began to play and as the bar got lower and lower, fewer and fewer people were left standing. It was amazing—obviously the hours I had spent going under the bar at high jump practice were paying off. At the end of the competition I was the last one standing (of course, it may have had something to do with my height, or lack thereof).

I may not have been the high jump champion, but I became the self-proclaimed limbo queen. What I believed had been an obstacle to my dream became an opportunity. By adjusting our perspective we can turn obstacles and challenges into opportunities to develop our potential.

Our ability to neutralize the power of potential-destroyers

in our life will determine whether we nurture or abort the seeds of greatness that are in us. It all comes down to what we believe about ourselves and about God.

Have you ever considered there may be a doctor, a lawyer, a humanitarian, a pastor, a politician, a scientist, a mom or dad, or a worship leader in you just waiting to be unleashed? You may even be called to invent the world's first instant, permanent, and pain-free hair remover! Never underestimate or undervalue the influence and impact your life can have on this generation and those to come.

Truth Over Facts

By the age of thirty-three there were some things that had been resolved in my life. I'd come through the difficult years of puberty when I was convinced my parents' main purpose in life was to make me miserable. I no longer had to spend every waking moment (or more accurately the entire night before a research paper was due) buried in books for school or college. I was married to an incredible (and very gorgeous) man, and my work was my passion. I was living the life of my dreams.

Finding out I was adopted was never in the game plan. You can never really be prepared for something like that. This caused me to question so many things regarding what

I thought and believed about life and myself. Through it all, there was never any doubt about my relationship with God. But working through my fears, insecurities, and feelings of rejection took a little more time.

In the months after finding out I was adopted people wanted me to share this story every time I spoke. Inevitably, after each meeting I would end up speaking to people who had been adopted, given up a child for adoption, or were the husbands, wives, or children of adoptees. These conversations began to spark a desire in me to find out more about my biological parents.

One day I had enough courage to pick up the phone and call the adoption agency to begin the search. After filling out the initial forms, I waited for them to be processed and the results sent to me. I was home alone when the documents arrived in a fairly nondescript envelope. Nervously I opened the package. In it was a social worker's report that was written just a few weeks before I came into the world. As I read the overview of my mother's condition I came to this entry:

> Her estimated date of confinement is October 3 and she plans to give the baby away on adoption. She does not seem to be too emotionally involved with the child. She seems to want to get it all over with and get back to work as soon as possible.

This was the most difficult thing I had ever read. I had so wanted to believe my mother was forced to make the decision she did, that deep down she really wanted me. This report shattered that illusion.

Dumbfounded, I picked up the envelope again and pulled out my original birth certificate. On it was listed my date of birth, the hospital in which I was born, and my weight and height. As I read on, there next to the word *Mother* was my biological mother's name. Directly underneath it, in the box where my father's name should have appeared was one simple word—*unknown.* I took a deep breath in an attempt to hold back the tears.

Even more devastating was what appeared next to the box where my name should have been recorded. Again there was no name—just the word *unnamed.* My heart sank as I slumped to the floor still holding the certificate in my hand. I was overwhelmed by emotion and overcome by feelings of abandonment and rejection. Was I so unwanted that my mother hadn't even given me a name?

It was then, kneeling on the floor with birth certificate in hand, that God so powerfully reminded me of the words of Isaiah 49:1: "The Lord has called me from the womb; from the body of my mother He has named my name." With this Scripture resounding in my mind I rose from the floor and grabbed my Bible. With it in one hand and my birth certificate in the other, I had a choice to make. Was I going to accept what the facts that appeared on my birth certificate said about my identity, or believe the Truth contained in the Word of God? I knew the decision I made at that point would affect the course of my destiny. The wrong response at that critical time would have allowed the enemy to steal, kill, and destroy my future.

Both my certificate and my Bible were just ink on paper—it would take as much faith to believe one as it would the other. But only one professed the Truth. I threw the certificate to the ground and began to confess Isaiah 49:1 until I believed it. My mother may not have named me but God certainly had. The Word is Truth—a force that's higher and more powerful than the facts of our circumstances.

This was not the only time I had to appropriate God's Word in my life. In the weeks following I was bombarded with thoughts like, *You were just an accident. You weren't wanted. You were never planned. You were a mistake. You have no value. God could never use you.*

In the midst of my struggle John 8:31-32 came to life in a new way:

If you abide in My word [hold fast to My teachings and live in accordance with them], you are truly my disciples. And you will know the Truth, and the Truth will set you free.

This taught me a powerful principle: the Truth of God's Word can set us free. In order to experience this freedom we must first be abiding in His Word. Many of us miss out on being free because we only have a vague knowledge of the Word, or we only refer to it occasionally. We don't make abiding in it a way of life. The key to freedom is knowing the Truth because it is Truth that will set us free.

We can become overwhelmed by the facts of our circumstances—whether relational, emotional, spiritual, physical, or financial—simply because we choose to abide in the facts rather than in the Truth. Changing where we choose to abide requires a conscious decision.

Even though my emotions were volatile after finding out about my adoption, and at times my mind seemed out of control, God always gave me the power to choose life over death. But the choice was mine to make.

> I call heaven and earth to witness this day against you that I have set before you life and death, the blessings and the curses; therefore choose life, that you and your descendants may live. (*Deuteronomy 30:19*)

People often ask me how I was able to process such a devastating fact. Sometimes I think my response disappoints them because they are looking for a spectacular answer. I tell them the secret was simply to choose life. In practice this meant I had to choose to abide in the Word of God. That means holding fast to His teachings and living in accordance with them even when my feelings and emotions were screaming to do the opposite. You don't have to be superhuman to do this—simply obedient.

God Is For Us

I remember asking God on several occasions if He really knew what He was doing when He decided to make Nick and me parents. We had a combined score of two and a half out of twenty on the baby aptitude test. The score was indicative of the fact that neither of us had spent much time around babies. But despite me not knowing the difference between an "all in one" and a "hole in one" (I later found out the former was an item of babies clothing) God obviously believed in our capabilities and parenting potential.

We believed God would miraculously help us get up to speed in the parenting field but this required an adjustment in our thinking (a rather large one actually). We needed to start thinking of ourselves as parents, not the childless, thirty-something, latte-drinking couple we were.

The greatest limitations to our life are not external (not our spouse, our mother, or our boss) but those we self-impose because of what we think. God wants to set us free from limited and contained thinking. To do this it's essential we start by changing the thoughts we think. Unless we change the way we think, nothing changes.

When it comes to our dreams our thinking is extremely powerful. Just like the control panel of an aircraft determines its flight path, our thoughts will either take us toward our destiny or away from it, propelling us into our future or anchoring us to our past.

We Are What We Think

Our mind is the control center of our life, and our thinking is the essence of who we are. Therefore our ability to achieve our dreams and fulfill our destiny is directly influenced by our thinking. How we think determines our responses, our ability to relate to others, our level of commitment, our priorities, and the dreams we will pursue. Proverbs 23:7 puts it this way: "As [a man] thinks in his heart, so is he." To see our dreams and potential actualized will take more than adjusting old habits. It's not about behavior modification—it's about heart transformation. God wants to change us from the inside out.

My mind was definitely the biggest battleground in my life.

I grew up the daughter of Greek immigrants, and for most of my childhood, I was told the greatest ambition for a woman was to get married and have many, many, many children. In fact, I was advised that a woman should not aspire to anything more than this, as doing so would be detrimental to her femininity (and future marriage prospects). My life's path was mapped out for me and my culture and tradition shaped my belief system and defined my value as a person.

This life may have sounded tempting if I lived in a little fishing village on a sun-drenched Greek island (note to self: must look into this for next vacation). This not being the case, I knew I had the potential to live a much bigger life. In order to have this life my thinking needed a drastic overhaul (and still needs a regular tune-up).

You Can Change Your Thinking

The good news for all of us is that it doesn't matter how our mind has been programmed by our past. We can change our future by reprogramming our thinking. I wish I could laser this truth into your brain—it's the most critical step in the process. Fulfilling our destiny and realizing our potential all begins in our mind. That's why the devil tries to bombard our thinking. Romans 12:2 tells us:

> Do not be conformed to this world (this age), [fashioned after and adapted to its external, superficial customs], but be transformed (changed) by the [entire] renewal of your mind [by its new ideals and its new attitude], so that you may prove [for yourselves] what is the good and acceptable and perfect will of God, even the thing which is good and acceptable and perfect [in His sight for you].

This Scripture makes it clear that in order to fulfill God's purpose for our life we cannot have the same thought processes, responses, and actions as the world. We must develop new patterns of thinking by using God's Word to renew our mind. God calls this process *transformation*.

When translated, the Greek word *transformed* means *metamorphosis*. This is the action that brings about change in the actual substance of a thing. One of my favorite books when I

was growing up was *The Very Hungry Caterpillar*. Now this little insect could eat! He consumed everything from apples to
cupcakes. Done eating, and twelve times his original size, the
caterpillar entered a cocoon to sleep things off. The best part
of the book was the final page where our little friend turned
into a stunning butterfly. That's metamorphosis.

In the same way, if we're to experience change in our very
nature, we need to enter the cocoon of the Word of God.
When you sit in your lounge room or your favorite chair
reading the Bible, think *caterpillar*. It's like you're spinning
your own spiritual cocoon.

It's in the confines of the cocoon that the unseen work is
done in the caterpillar. This results in change to its very substance causing it to become a butterfly. This metamorphosis
is the external manifestation of an internal process. This is
exactly what happens to us when we abide in the Word of
God. It's here He can do His greatest work in us. As we
commit to this process we too will experience internal transformation that in time will cause external change.

Stay on Track

I used to catch the train to college. Every day the train was
scheduled to leave at 8:30 A.M. from platform one. I always

checked the departure schedule as it seemed every other day the train was delayed or there was a strike or problem with the train line.

On one occasion, I was running late and jumped on a train without checking the schedule. Although it left from my usual platform and at the usual time, this train was going to the wrong destination. Consequently so was I! I got off the train at the next station and marched up to the stationmaster to express my frustration about the unreliability of the public transport system. He politely listened to my protest and then reminded me it was I who boarded the wrong train.

Our thoughts are just like a train . . . they will always take us somewhere. They will either take us toward our destination (our destiny) or away from it. We are bombarded daily with thoughts of fear, doubt, negativity, offence, unforgiveness, and bitterness, but we don't have to board these thoughts. If we do we will end up in a place we don't want to be—destinations like anger, jealousy, confusion, or self-pity. Instead we can choose to jump aboard a train of thought that will take us to a place of love, joy, peace, and happiness.

We must be committed to the daily process of renewing our mind to ensure our thinking is not derailed. Even if we have boarded the wrong train of thought, the great news is we can disembark at any time. Second Corinthians 10:5 reveals we can

[R]efute arguments and theories and reasonings and every proud and lofty thing that sets itself up against the [true] knowledge of God; and . . . lead every thought and purpose away captive into the obedience of Christ (the Messiah, the Anointed One).

We have the power to arrest our thinking. We don't have to stay miserable, depressed, or angry if we're willing to get off that train of thought and jump on board the right thoughts.

Just in case you're wondering what the right kind of thoughts are, the Apostle Paul gives us some tips:

Whatever is true, whatever is worthy of reverence and is honorable and seemly, whatever is just, whatever is pure, whatever is lovely and lovable, whatever is kind and winsome and gracious, if there is any virtue and excellence, if there is anything worthy of praise, think on and weigh and take account of these things [fix your minds on them]. *(Philippians 4:8)*

In terms of my adoption this Scripture translated itself in a very practical way. I had to discover the good that could come from all of this (I wasn't sure there was anything good). Then I had to choose to think about those things instead of thoughts like, *Why was I lied to?* or *Why did my mother reject me?* If I hadn't changed my thinking I would have remained an emotional mess.

As I searched for the good, I recalled a conversation I had with my mom's neighbor not long after I found out about my adoption. Thirty-five years earlier my mother had been sitting in this neighbor's backyard. Their talk was interrupted by yells from the other side of the fence. Recognizing the voice, my mom ran toward the sound. "We've got a girl! We've got a girl!" my grandmother announced excitedly to the entire neighborhood after getting off the phone with the adoption agency. My mother stood up and ran to my grandmother's side overcome by joy. The news the entire family had anxiously been awaiting had finally arrived. A little girl would be coming home soon and her name would be Christina. (I don't think they even knew my name meant "follower of Christ." How prophetic that proved to be.)

One of the most powerful truths I could hold on to was that my family had especially chosen me. I had to make the decision to cling to this truth daily (sometimes hourly). As I focused on this truth rather than the thought that I was unwanted by my biological mother, I could continue to move toward my destiny and not be crippled by rejection and hurt.

Whatever we're facing there's always something positive to consider. Don't allow what is not happening in your marriage, career, ministry, finances, or relationships to direct your thoughts. Instead look to God's Word and His promises—focus on these. Our ability to change the way we think about

God and ourselves will shape the future we'll have. It's only by renewing our mind and aligning our thinking to the Word of God that we'll give birth to our dreams.

§

Believe

Yep, the belief journey has been a big one for me because so much came out of what I was allowing myself to believe—the Truth or the facts. I'm hoping to save you some time (and angst) by sharing a quick list of principles I only realized the importance of in hindsight.

1. Make the Word Your Greatest Weapon

One of the necessities for this first step is a Bible! You may not have used yours for a while, but I want to encourage you to take it down from the bookshelf, dust it off, and open it. As long as it stays closed your biggest weapon against unbelief and the lies the enemy wants to convince you of goes unused.

➤ Choose to believe the Word—Even if it's hard to believe, make the decision to do it.
➤ Write it down—Put it on the fridge (this is of particular help if you're trying to give up dessert), on your bath-

room mirror, or stick it on the windshield of your car—wherever you can see it regularly.

➤ Continually confess the Word—Speaking it out will stir your faith.

➤ When all else fails keep standing on it—The Word is a great platform for victory.

2. Make the Faith of Others a Motivator

The faith-walk of others can inspire us to believe that maybe we can do it too. Although I can't imagine what it would be like to spend a lifetime cleaning the wounds of lepers and helping the lame in India (my challenge would be with the fact there is no running water in many places), Mother Teresa's story helps me believe that maybe, just maybe I can do half as much for humanity in my lifetime as she did.

➤ Read the stories of Christians and non-Christians who have achieved great things.

➤ Surround yourself with people who love Jesus and are living for Him.

3. Make Your Future Your Friend

It wasn't until I was willing to sever myself from wrong thinking, wrong beliefs, and past hurts that I could truly believe that God had great things waiting for me in my future.

Nothing, and I mean nothing, has to keep us out of this future. Ask yourself:

➤ What about the future scares me?
➤ What relationships might inhibit me from pursuing God's plan for my life?
➤ Do I really believe God's plan is the best plan for my life?

Section 3

ENVISION

✺ Diary Entry

I'm sure the doctors were trying to prepare me for the pain of labor by making me sit in a waiting room for half an hour after drinking twelve glasses of water! Nick and I were waiting—patiently—for our first ultrasound. As I sat there I wondered how many women were sent home and forced to reschedule because they could not resist the lure of the bathroom.

Just as I was thinking that rescheduling wouldn't be so bad, the nurse called out our names. She led us into the room where the sonographer, with the ultrasound thingy (I never can remember what they call it; all I know is it's cold) put the jelly on my tummy. She began to maneuver the thingy over my stomach as Nick and I looked at the screen intently—pretending we actually could see a baby in the mass of black swirls—only to be told that was my pan-

creas, not the baby. We both nodded but we knew our mistake was an easy one to make. It all looks so alike in there!

Soon the doctor picked up the baby's heartbeat. A little afraid of making the same mistake twice I held back my excitement in case I was actually looking at my bladder. To help us out the doctor was kind enough to put little signs on the screen: head, elbow, foot, heart, kidneys . . . how amazing. There he was making his screen debut—baby DJ!

We were so sure we were having a boy. We had received a prophetic word two years before so we didn't hesitate when asked if we wanted to know the baby's sex.

Sonographer: "It's a girl!"

Me: "Please check again." (Not for the life of me could I understand how she could determine the baby's gender in that black blur!)

Sonographer: "No, it's definitely a girl."

But the prophetic word! All this time we have been calling her DJ. I hope we haven't given her an identity complex!

See the Dream

As Nick and I waited for our ultrasound—me feeling like I had consumed half the world's water supply—we knew that seeing our baby would somehow make her more real. Seeing her would also help me believe I wasn't merely delusional—something was preventing me from stomaching anything other than toast.

The ultrasound pictures of our little girl went straight up on the wall (we were going to put them on the refrigerator but I could not get within ten feet of it without gagging). Looking at these pictures constantly helped Nick and I envision our little girl and kept us future-focused.

The snapshots reminded us that in five months our world was going to look dramatically different, and our life would be much more exciting. Although there was still a long (and sometimes very painful) road ahead, the picture motivated us to keep pressing on.

Envisioning our dream will keep us focused and on track to do whatever it takes to see it realized. Viktor Frankl, a successful Viennese psychiatrist who spent three years in

Nazi concentration camps, was a living testimony of the power of a dream. In a speech he gave after his release he said,

> There is only one reason why I am here today. What kept me alive was you. Others gave up hope. I dreamed. I dreamed that someday I would be here, telling you how I, Viktor Frankl, had survived the Nazi concentration camps. I've never been here before, I've never seen any of you before, I've never given this speech before. But in my dreams, I have stood before you and said these words a thousand times.

There is power in envisioning a dream. For Viktor Frankl, the ability to dream about a hope beyond the horrific atrocities he experienced during World War II helped keep him alive. It was the dream of Martin Luther King Jr. that fueled an end to segregation in the United States. It was a dream that gave Mother Teresa the strength to help bring dignity to thousands of India's poor and marginalized. And it was a dream that helped Nelson Mandela survive political imprisonment and eventually bring an end to apartheid in South Africa.

Nick and I visited Robbin Island, where Nelson Mandela was imprisoned for eighteen years for believing his people should have freedom. I walked down the narrow hallway toward the door of what was once his cell. I began to weep, overwhelmed by the Spartan conditions. The cell was tiny and dark. Every night for the first six years Mandela slept on the cold concrete floor. Some time later, he was afforded the luxury of a six-inch-thick mattress. It was difficult to imagine how anyone could survive such conditions.

The prison has now been turned into a museum. Our guide that day had spent time in jail with Mandela. When asked what Mandela was like in prison his response was astounding.

"Mr. Mandela was just the same as you see today, always full of joy and hope. In fact we frequently had to ask him if he actually realized he was in prison."

As the guide relayed this story I wondered how anyone in this depressing environment could think about anything but his or her containment. Then it came to me. It was Mandela's ability to envision a free and equal South Africa (his dream) that kept him free and alive on the inside regardless of his external circumstances. What a powerful and inspiring image of a man driven by his dream.

Anyone whose life has impacted the world started with a dream. Their dream unearthed the potential that was always inside them and provided a framework for their potential to be actualized.

In the same way, a commitment to our dreams will unlock the potential that's in us. Our dream may be a business idea or invention, a humanitarian cause, or a ministry to which we want to devote our life. It may have more to do with the kind of mother, father, or friend we want to be. It may be staying fit and healthy so we can enjoy the latter years of our life (and our grandkids). Whatever the size of our dream, envisioning or focusing on it will give us the ability to do and overcome anything in order to see it become a reality.

I dreamed of achieving something significant for God but because of my Greek Orthodox upbringing, and paradigm of Christianity, the only thing I thought a woman could do in ministry was become a nun (I don't know how I would have survived a three-day silent retreat!). Then one day I walked into Hillsong Church. Preaching that day was one of our female pastors. I was stunned. I had never before seen a woman do what she was doing. I thought you had to be a priest to be allowed to speak at the front of a church!

That day I got a glimpse of what I believed I was called to do—preach the Gospel. Before seeing my dream I always knew there had to be more to life than going to a university, working a job, getting married, and having children (all of which are good things, but for me not the only things). There was a deep yearning in my heart to preach, but I didn't know how to give it expression because I had never seen a woman do it before. I didn't know exactly what it would take to achieve this dream, but fueled by the vision of my future I immersed myself in church life. I listened to every Christian tape I could find. I read scores of books and enrolled in Bible college.

My willingness to do whatever it took to realize my dream, and my hunger for the things of God, were like magnets attracting opportunity. It came in the form of a request from our assistant youth pastor to help start a youth center in our community. I was so thrilled to be asked. I did not need three confirmations and a personal visitation from an angel in order to say yes. It was my passion for God that sealed my decision.

And my dream grew.

In time I became the director of that same youth center.

And my dream grew.

I then became the state director of a national youth movement.

And my dream grew.

Today my family and I travel to every continent in the world (okay, except Antarctica) preaching the Gospel.

And my dream continues to grow.

Who would have believed that a Greek girl from the western suburbs of Sydney, with a dream to see people come into relationship with Jesus, would have the incredible opportunity to travel the world, preach the Gospel, and see people won into the Kingdom of God? All of this started with a dream.

At the time my decision to volunteer at the youth center

seemed insignificant. It wasn't very glamorous or spectacular, particularly when a young person who had had a little too much to drink decided to vomit on my shoe. Painting walls at 2:00 A.M., cleaning toilets, administration, and writing funding proposals so we could keep the doors open was not always exciting. But it was during my six years there that I developed the skills and character necessary to do what I'm doing today. And it's there I learned how to dream bigger dreams.

Did I have the ability to communicate when I was mopping the bathroom floors? Yes, and God always saw nations for my life. But He was using this process to build me on the inside. He taught me about submission, faith, loyalty, commitment, endurance, faithfulness, generosity, and how to do it all on five hours' sleep a night!

It's these qualities that now underpin all aspects of my life—family, relationships, church, ministry, and my personal walk with God. Although many of the tasks I did at the youth center seemed far removed from my dream of communicating God's Truth to a generation, they were all very necessary. He was building a foundation in me that would ensure He could achieve His purposes through me. I genuinely believe I would have not only missed what God had for me if I had despised my time at the center, but also run the risk of aborting my dream altogether.

People often ask me what it takes to do what I'm doing today. I tell them that if they're not willing to walk through the embryo stage there will never come a baby. I encourage them to start serving and doing whatever needs to be done (yes, even if that's changing the toilet rolls between church services). Although right now this may seem ordinary or small, God can take the seemingly insignificant and unspectacular and use it spectacularly.

Take the disciples for example, an eclectic mix of men from all walks and backgrounds. Some were fisherman, some politicians, and one was a tax collector. None of them started life as world changers. They were simply willing to follow Jesus. In three years Jesus led and trained these men, transforming them so much that He left the evangelization of the world up to them. Almost two thousand years later their impact is still being felt daily throughout the globe.

Great people don't start out great. It begins with the seed of a dream accompanied by lots and lots of apparently small, seemingly inconsequential choices that collectively lead to the realization of that dream.

The Power of Planning

If we want to live a life of significance we need to understand that it won't happen by accident. We must be intentional about the choices we make in relation to our dreams, and set goals to ensure we are moving toward them daily.

Another question I'm regularly asked is how I balance marriage, motherhood, and ministry (a whole other book), and keep my sanity. The truth is my God-given dream fuels me; therefore my life is very focused and uncomplicated. I plan my time according to my priorities rather than letting my life just happen. Most of the year I work hard traveling and speaking. But as important as it is to book my tickets or organize my speaking schedule, it's no less important to plan dinner dates with my husband, go to the beach or park with my daughter, see a movie with friends, and keep fit and healthy.

Many people live life going with the flow or taking life as it comes. They have no strategy or infrastructure in place to facilitate the realization of their dream. The fact is, when it comes to fulfilling our destiny we can't hit a target we cannot see. Studies show that those people who have written measurable goals and plans are more likely to succeed than those who don't. In fact, one of the primary factors associated with underachievement is confusion and fuzziness when it comes to goals. Goals, accompanied by a burning desire to see them accomplished, dramatically increase the probability we'll achieve our dreams (within reason that is— marrying the future king of England is not impossible, but very unlikely).

As I pursued my dreams I set very specific goals along the

way. I understood that only a succession of small, daily, measured steps would take me into the future I envisioned. Of course this was coupled with God's favor, anointing, and opportunity.

It's not enough to see the future we want; we have to be deliberate about the actions we take to make this future a reality. We need to ask ourselves, "What future do I see for myself, my family, my relationships, my work, my finances, and my ministry?" We need to start envisioning ourselves in the future we want to have, and begin to take small, incremental steps (even if they don't look like much) toward that dream. In the words of the prophet Zechariah, "Do not despise . . . small beginnings" (see Zechariah 4:10 NLT).

The Impossible Is Possible

After the prophetic word regarding the gender of my child, it took me a few moments to process the fact that the baby I was carrying was a girl. I thought this baby was that boy prophesied. I was thrilled I was having a girl, just a little surprised is all. I realized I had a predetermined picture of what my baby was going to look like. Clearly what I saw was different than what God was seeing. He obviously had much more planned for me than I originally thought (I couldn't allow my mind to think about a second baby . . . I hadn't even given birth to the first one yet!). God's thinking was definitely bigger than mine. In the wake of the ultrasound, Isaiah 55:8-9 held new relevance for me.

> For my thoughts are not your thoughts, neither are your ways My ways, says the Lord. For as the heavens are higher than the earth, so are My ways higher than your ways and My thoughts than your thoughts.

God's perspective on our life and future is more extensive than ours. Where our view might be distorted or limited, God's view is clear. The picture we see for our future is often based on our experiences, resources, expectations, socioeconomic background, traditions, education, and culture. But God is not limited by these.

- Where we see lack, God sees opportunity.
- Where we see failure, God sees potential.
- Where we see containment, God sees refinement.
- Where we see weakness, God sees strength.
- Where we see death, God sees life.
- Where we see what is or has been, God sees what can and will be.

To see our dreams realized, our perspective has to come in line with God's. For four months I had referred to the bump in my stomach as our little boy. Once I realized my perspective was wrong, *he* became *she,* and I started thinking dresses and hair ribbons instead of sports clothes and footballs. When we commit to seeing our life through God's eyes, even if what we're facing seems impossible or our dreams are out of reach, we can be confident that "all things are possible with God" (Matthew 19:26). Maybe even twins.

We only have to look in the Bible to know this is true. It's filled with stories of people facing impossible situations. When God came into the equation these people were able to achieve the seemingly impossible. Think about Moses. When God asked him to lead the Israelites to freedom after years of oppression Moses protested, "But God I'm not eloquent enough and no one will listen to me" (see Exodus 4:10). God still used Moses mightily. When God called Jeremiah to become a prophet to the nations his initial response was, "But God I cannot speak for I am only a youth" (see Jeremiah 1:6). God still used Jeremiah mightily. When Gideon was asked to be Israel's deliverer he said, "But God I'm the least of the least" (see Judges 6:15). God still used Gideon mightily.

These men responded to God's call with a list of self-proclaimed limitations as if their weaknesses were unknown by God when He called them! In order for these men to fulfill their destiny they had to have a serious "but-ectomy" (you won't find that one in your medical dictionary). They had to leave their "buts" behind and trust that God could make the impossible possible. The fact is most of us respond to God in exactly the same way—with our big "buts" (and I'm not talking about needing to get on a treadmill). For example, here are a few of the "buts" I've tried with God.

"But, God, I'm Greek."
God's response: "I like Greeks."

I was brought up in a culture where a jar of olive oil was considered a low-fat diet, and a light snack was a four-course meal. At family functions we would break plates while others ate off them. Immediate family included anyone up to a third cousin, and everything we did was loud.

Within the confines of the Greek community it was good being Greek. Actually it was more than good. My relatives believed Greek culture was the bedrock of all things civilized. However, outside this environment prejudice became obvious. At school the other kids would laugh at me because, while they had peanut butter and jelly sandwiches, I had olives, feta cheese, and salami (the aroma was potent and I was regularly reminded of this fact by the other kids).

Growing up I wondered how a Greek girl could ever do anything significant for God. My dreams were in direct opposition to the acceptable life path for a Greek woman— marry young, have children, and set up house. These were great things, but not the only things God had for me.

Although there were times I believed my ethnicity was an obstacle to my future, it was no challenge for God (after all, He made me Greek). I had to choose to place my dream over my culture and tradition. God didn't want me to totally discard all elements of being Greek, only those things that would hold me back from my destiny. Breaking ties with the only tradition I had known was difficult but essential if I was to embrace all God had for me.

"But, God, I'm a girl."
God's response: "Christine, I didn't fail biology."

I can still hear my mom's voice. "Christina, how many times do I have to tell you girls don't play soccer? Boys don't like rough girls, and for you to get married, the boys need to see you in the kitchen cooking."

I always thought it was so unfair that the boys could play all the fun games while the girls were relegated to playing with dolls. (I know this sounds outdated, but growing up my world was defined by very clear gender roles.) One year I ran home with my report card only to be told, "You don't need brains to get married and have children, Christina. No man will want you if he thinks you are smarter than him."

I was constantly reminded not to set my sights too high because, as a woman, there was only so much I could do. It was as if my gender was a limitation for me fulfilling the purposes of God for my life—a lid on all the hopes, dreams, and gifts locked up inside of me.

If I was going to live my dreams I had to put aside everything I assumed about women and discover what God actually said about women. As I read the Bible I was stunned to discover that God not only believed in women, He had used them powerfully to make a difference in the world. Throughout history women have been culturally limited by their gender. At times even the Church has oppressed women due to tradition. However, Jesus Christ is one of the greatest emancipators (that's just a big word for someone who brings freedom) of women to ever walk the planet.

I soon realized that gender roles were instituted by culture and tradition, not by God. In Him we are two sexes but one race. Women were there from the beginning of creation, not a mere afterthought or appendage to the body of Christ. We were made intentionally to complete His body, and together with men we reflect the true image of God. We're equal, but different (Amen to that! Can you imagine how boring life would be if we were all the same?).

I never believed a woman could do what I'm doing today, but as I have remained obedient to God's call, I'm amazed by the opportunities He has opened up for me. Gender is not an obstacle to fulfilling our destiny. Our sex is no surprise to God; He knew it when He determined our purpose.

"But, God, I'm twenty-nine and not married."
God's response: "Husband or not,
you have a destiny."

In many Greek families, turning eighteen is a milestone for women because it means they can get married. Whenever I visited any of my relatives they tried to marry me off to the next eligible Greek boy—only I was never very interested.

When I was twenty and still single, my uncles would urge me to hurry up and find someone because, "all of the really good ones will be gone." When I was single at twenty-four, they would say, "Christina, it's okay, some boy will still have you; don't give up hope." By the time I was twenty-seven and still single, I could hear the whispers before I walked into a room. "Here she comes. No one bring up marriage—the poor girl has been left on the shelf; no one wants her. It's because of her progressive ideas and her religion. If she was just normal she would be married by now."

For many years I was led to believe my value and identity would only be found in my husband and in my role as a wife and mother (even with my cooking deficiency). I have since discovered that, regardless of marital status, our identity only comes from Christ. Being single didn't have to be a hindrance to my dreams. Nor would my commitment to the things of God scare off the man with whom I was supposed to spend the rest of my life. In fact, the only way I would end up with this man was if I kept pursuing my destiny relentlessly. People (often Christians) would tell me to slow down or pull back, concerned that at the pace I was running I would never meet a man. Thank God I never really listened to them, because Nick just happened to be running as hard for God as I was when our lives collided. After the God-orchestrated encounter (it had to be God because I was the self-proclaimed president of the "Single Till the Rapture Club") we realized we were going the same way and decided to finish the race together.

If I had taken my friends' advice or wasted my time sitting around waiting for my knight in shining armor to ride into my life, I would never have laid the foundation in my twenties for what I'm doing today, and Nick would have probably run right past me.

Whether single, married, divorced, or widowed, God has a purpose for us in each season of life. Rather than viewing singleness as an obstacle to fulfilling our God-given destiny, or marriage as an excuse for pulling back from the purposes of God, we need to passionately embrace the life God has given us.

"But, God, I'm from a public housing project."
God's response: "I know your address."

When I was growing up my suburb wasn't the kind of place you wanted on your resume. Like many immigrants to Australia at that time, my family lived in public housing. Back then substance abuse, high rates of unemployment, teenage pregnancy, and crime defined the area in which I lived.

It wasn't until I enrolled in a university that I realized just what others thought about my suburb and the people who lived in it. As I stood in the enrollment line I overheard the conversation of the girls standing in front of me. They were obviously from a private school and I was feeling a little intimidated by the quality of their speech. After a while one of the girls asked me where I was from. As I answered her question I noticed the girls stepping away from me seemingly gripped by fear. Stone-faced they asked, "Do you carry a knife or a gun?" It took everything in me to stop myself from falling over with laughter.

I could have allowed these stereotypes and views about where I grew up to limit me and prevent me from pursuing my destiny. Instead I chose to rise above them and follow my dreams. You may believe that how much you can achieve is limited by where you grew up, where you went to school, who you know (or don't know), or the fact you live in the middle of nowhere and think that God could never find you. How wrong you are. God knew your address and all the circumstances of your life when He called you and planted dreams in your heart. As for locating you, God knows every house (including every tent, hut, and igloo) on every street in every city around the globe. He forgets no one.

Where we live, our culture, tradition, or our socioeconomic background, doesn't have to limit our future. If God can use someone like me, He can use you too. We all have the power to change the future. Don't let your "buts" prevent you from pursuing the purposes of God for your life. God-dreams are impossible to achieve in our own strength (this ensures that God always gets the glory). If we're to see the supernatural doors of provision and opportunity open in our lives, we must first believe that our dreams, as impossible as they may seem, are possible. In the words of Pastor Tommy Barnett, "You only know a dream is from God if it freaks you out in its impossibility."ii

Envision

Without renewed vision I now know I would be thinking the same way, living the same way, and doing the same things as I did before I met Jesus (very scary concept). I thank God for people, an environment, and a Saviour that helped enlarge what I was seeing. If we fail to expand our vision we too run the risk of getting stuck in the smallness of the life we've lived to this point. Remember, God has so much more for you. Here are some tips on how to develop a bigger perspective.

1. Take Time to Step Back

We have all heard the saying: "You can't see the forest for the trees." When it comes to life and our dreams, we too can get so immersed in the routine of life—work, marriage, kids, church, and study—that we lose focus of the *why* of our existence. Losing our focus can reduce life to a set of tasks that we have to get through, stealing our passion and our drive.

➤ Pause—Take time (now I'm not talking six months on the Caribbean) to look at where you're at.

➤ Assess—What does your life look like and where are you focusing?

➤ Ask God—To help you realign your vision to the plan He has for you.

2. Take Your Eyes Off Your Navel

Some people enjoy looking at the stars, some love origami, but for others navel gazing has become their favorite pastime. As long as our focus is on our navel—our needs, our situation, and our wants—we will never see the promises of God for our life because we are too busy looking downward.

➤ Pause—This is a good time to determine how much time you spend looking at your feet.

➤ Assess—Are you more focused on your needs and wants than God's needs and wants?

➤ Ask God—To help you lift your head and show you that there is much more to see than the lint in your belly button.

3. Take a Larger Look at Life

A friend of mine recently told me many New Yorkers are nearsighted because they spend their life surrounded by big buildings and never use their long-range vision (whether this is medical fact or merely a good story I'm not sure!). In the context of our dreams, seeing only that which is directly before us can cause spiritual shortsightedness. Yes, it's important to focus on the opportunities we have in our hand today, but a long-range vision for our lives will keep us moving forward and cause us to step out and take risks.

➤ Pause—Take a drive to the highest point in your city to get a picture of how broad a vision God wants you to have.
➤ Assess—How high, wide, and far you are seeing. Are you seeing just today, this week, or this year, or can you envision a lifetime?
➤ Ask God—To give you new vision and add clarity to what He has already shown you.

Section 4

POSITION

✿ Diary Entry

Healthy Baby 101

- *Must cut out coffee (this is more painful than I expected).*
- *Must not consume soft cheeses like the moldy blue-vein ones.*
- *Must stay away from negative people.*
- *Must play worship music as I'm falling asleep.*
- *Must speak only in smooth, soft tones so I won't startle baby.*
- *Must be in church always so baby gets a glimpse (or at least hears a glimpse) of what her life is going to be like.*
- *Must talk to tummy always and must ensure Nick talks to tummy always (other than in public places).*
- *Pray for baby.*
- *Pray for pain-free birth.*
- *Pray that labor will last no more than four hours.*
- *Pray for no epidural (or pray for one depending on how painful labor really is).*

- *Pray that one day I will be able to eat again without feeling like I'm about to throw up.*
- *Pray I will survive the fifteen overseas trips scheduled before the baby is born (at least morning sickness gives me a viable excuse for not eating dreaded plane food . . . I always feel so guilty for not even taking one bite).*
- *Pray I'll be able to survive this whole thing without the aid of caffeine.*

Be Willing to Flex

No one told me I would have to give up everything I really liked eating in order to go up three dress sizes! But living without coffee, cheese, and chocolate for eight months (the first month didn't count because I had no idea I was pregnant) was a small price to pay to ensure our little girl would receive the best start in life.

I not only had to watch what I ate, I was also acutely aware of the environments in which I found myself. I did not want to do anything that would pose a risk to the baby's health, particularly in the first trimester of my pregnancy (my trusty pregnancy guide said this is when babies are most at risk). Although God was ultimately in control, I had a responsibility to do all I could to nurture and protect the seed I was carrying in my womb. I became very conscious of the potential of the life growing inside of me, and I knew everything I did would affect her (no pressure!). I began to gravitate toward things that would help with her development. I played worship music constantly; I read Bible stories to my tummy; and I drank freshly squeezed juices (even the ones that tasted like mud) believing they might do her (and me) some good.

Our dreams, too, are vulnerable in the early stages of development. If we're not conscious of the need to protect and nurture them, they may be miscarried or aborted. (Remember this is more likely when they're still in seed form.) We need to evaluate every aspect of our life and determine what habits, behaviors, people, and places will help grow our dreams, and which ones might jeopardize them. This is the only way our dreams will come to pass. We must have the courage to let go of the things that would hinder our destiny and embrace those that will help unlock our potential.

My primary objective during pregnancy was to give birth to a healthy baby. Although adjustment was not always easy or pleasurable, I was prepared to do it for my baby's sake.

Adjust Our Consumption Habits

I'm a café latte sort of chick and I love a good, strong coffee. Shortly after becoming pregnant I was told caffeine wasn't good for the baby, that it could in fact impede her development. Enough said! I not only stopped drinking coffee, I removed any temptation by giving my coffeemaker and all the coffee in the house away (Nick was also forced into coffee exile by association). I avoided my daily visits to Starbucks and devised creative techniques to complete a devotional time without falling asleep. What I couldn't understand was why pickles and ice cream were fine to eat (at 2:00 in the morning) while coffee and sushi were off the menu (who makes these decisions?). Nevertheless, I obediently adhered to the seemingly universal pregnancy diet guide because I did not want to jeopardize my baby.

When it comes to our dreams, we too have to adjust our consumption habits if our dreams are to fully mature. Our eyes and ears are the gateways to our heart—just as our mouth is to our stomach—and our dreams flow from our heart. This is the reason the Bible tells us we need to guard what enters our heart—in other words what we're eating. Proverbs 4:23 puts it a little more eloquently: "Keep and guard your heart with all vigilance and above all that you guard, for out of it flow the springs of life."

What we allow to enter our heart will greatly influence who we'll become. As a new Christian, I had no idea I had to control what entered my heart. I continued in my old patterns of behavior. I watched the same things, read the same things, and spent time with the same people. I maintained the same diet of negativity, gossip, and doubt and wondered why I was not growing in the purposes of God.

In time I became aware I had to change certain things in

order to grow (listening to all those sermons helped). I began to limit the TV programs and movies I watched. I replaced magazines with the Bible and Christian books. And I listened to preaching tapes instead of the radio in my car (okay, most of the time). In our world of mass media it's often difficult to escape the daily bombardment of information, but we do have the power to filter what we absorb. If we put good things in we can expect good results (think fiber).

On the flip side, a bad diet will eventually kill our dreams. It's essential that we constantly evaluate the nutritional value of what we are feeding ourselves. It may come down to how many hours of television we're viewing, the quality of the programs we're watching, what music we're listening to, the material we're reading, the conversations we're having, the movies we're seeing, the Web sites we're visiting, the video games we're playing, or the people with whom we're associating. As harmless as these may sometimes seem, excessive consumption of things that induce negative thinking, bad habits, and wrong behavior will thwart our potential.

A good litmus test is to ask yourself if you're giving more airtime to the media, educators, politicians, economists, pop stars, friends, or tradition than you are to God's Word. To see our dreams actualized, God's Word and His will must take precedence over everything else.

Surround Ourselves with Dreamers

I've often heard it said, "Where we end up in life will be determined by the people we associate with and the books we read." For now I just want to focus on the first part of that thought. Whatever our dreams are, our relationships with others will take us toward our dreams or away from them. Right relationships are crucial for the fulfillment of our dreams.

Before I was pregnant I hardly ever noticed pregnant women, but once I had joined the ranks of mothers-to-be it seemed every second woman I met was about to have a baby. My relationships to that point were mostly with people who didn't have children. Although they were great friends they couldn't help me with the finer points of pregnancy or raising kids. In order to build my motherhood potential I had to proactively seek out relationships with other moms. I couldn't expect to learn all I needed to know for the next season of my life from people who hadn't been there before me. I had to be prepared to enlarge my world and develop new relationships with women who could offer some great advice (who else could understand what it's like to feel like a beach ball and not be able to see your feet for months?).

Right relationships are also imperative when it comes to

our dreams. We need to seek out relationships with those people who are further along the journey than we are. These are people who know how to motivate, inspire, and challenge us. They're there to celebrate our successes, walk with us through our disappointments, and ask us the hard questions to help us stay on track.

Often God will bring people into our lives who are very different from us to help unearth our undeveloped potential. God desires that we continually grow—body, soul, and spirit. Our relationships will help this process. A diversity of relationships will develop various facets of our life. It's often difficult to step out of our comfort zone to build relationships with people who are different from us, but it's critical that we do. If we only build relationships with people who are like us, we'll limit our potential for growth.

One person God has used powerfully in my life is my friend Holly Wagner. Although Holly lives in Los Angeles, California, and I live in Sydney, Australia (for those of us who failed geography, these cities are on opposite sides of the planet), we have developed an incredible relationship. We share our highs and lows, and inspire and encourage each other on the journey.

This did not happen overnight. Any relationship that will move us toward our destiny will take an ongoing investment of time, emotion, and resources. For Holly and I this includes her visiting me at the LAX airport when I have a layover, and me rearranging my schedule whenever she's in Australia to ensure we make time to catch up. We are also in frequent contact via telephone and e-mail. (How did people live before the Internet and cell phones?)

When Holly came into my life we were very different (we still are). She was always immaculately dressed, brightly coordinated, and looked great. I, on the other hand, had a wardrobe consisting of every variation of the color black. I also perfected the wash and shake look when it came to my hair. And makeup—let's not mention makeup!

I wasn't very confident in this area of my life, and I saw a freedom I wanted in the way Holly dressed and carried herself. This may seem like a strange desire. But it was actually an important step in my journey to wholeness, as aspects of my past had affected me both internally and externally. Who better to help me develop this side of my potential than Holly!

I will never forget the first shopping trip she took (dragged) me on. She made me try on what seemed to be every fuchsia, pastel, or paisley article of clothing ever created. I looked like wallpaper on legs! I was almost hyperventilating because all I wanted to do was to put my black suit back on and leave the pastel world far, far behind. Noticing the blood had drained from my face, Holly quickly understood I wasn't quite ready for a total external overhaul. Rather than try to make me a Holly clone (since there is about a foot difference in our height, this was going to prove difficult anyway) she had to accept where I was and settle for the revolutionary concept of a red shirt under my suit as the first step in my journey.

I have come a long way since that shopping expedition. My wardrobe now consists of many colors, including a paisley shirt or two. I thank God that Holly not only accepted me as I was but is still helping me to become all I can be. She is just one of many people I have in my life. Although all my friends are different, they each help develop an aspect of my potential (and I, theirs). Some are involved in my day-to-day life, while others inspire and influence me from a distance through their example and teaching resources. The common thread in all these relationships is our passion for God and our commitment to pursuing His purposes.

Not one of us will fulfill our destiny alone. Godly relationships will help grow, replenish, and refuel us so we can continually move closer to our dreams. Besides, it's so much more fun doing life together! We need to ensure we have friends we can pray with, talk candidly with, be accountable to, and be mentored by (even from a distance). It's critical that we constantly evaluate whom we're in relationships with to ensure they're taking us toward our dreams and not holding us back from our destinies.

Keep Our World Healthy

Early in my pregnancy I found out my friend's daughter had measles. I frantically called my mom and then my doctor to find out if this posed a risk to my unborn baby. Their advice (my mom's was a little more fervent than my doctor's) was to stay away. So, just to be sure, I didn't go within fifteen miles of her for two weeks.

Just as there were some places that posed a risk to my pregnancy, there are also environments that can threaten our dreams. Some of these environments may have been okay before we became pregnant with our dream, but now they can be destructive.

It amazes me how differently I reacted to my environment once I was carrying a baby. I felt so responsible for the baby's well-being. I avoided places and conversations that might be full of fear, doubt, negativity, or gossip, because I didn't want my unborn child to be exposed to these things (I didn't know how much of it she could hear, but I wanted to be sure I had all my bases covered).

I had to take similar action in the early stage of my dream. I remember when family gatherings (and there were so many of them) were the bane of my life because I knew my dreams would get a battering while I was there. My family's favorite dinner pastime was to joke about my dream of working in full-time ministry. They could not understand why anyone, particularly someone who had a university degree, would want to become a nun (my mom found it difficult to picture me in a convent). I remember leaving these dinners feeling deflated and depleted.

I soon recognized that in order for my dream to survive I had to limit how many family dinners I attended. This was a very difficult decision to make because I love my family and I'm very close to them. I felt the pain and loneliness of having to cut back my visits (incidentally, I also lost a lot of weight), but for a season it was vital. Adjustment was imperative in order to sustain my dream.

As my dream grew, family dinners no longer were a threat because my dream was strong enough to survive the ridicule. In fact, as my family saw aspects of my dream gradually realized, the criticism and negativity stopped. They even began to admire my life. Today our relationship is stronger than ever.

Like me, you too will face your own dream-threatening environments. It may be going to the pub or the local nightclub or joining in on the lunchroom gossip. Perhaps it's being around certain family and friends for extended periods of time or around mediocre, apathetic Christians who have grown stale. Whatever it is, if it takes us away from fulfilling our purpose, we must have the courage to walk away from these environments for the sake of our dreams.

It's also imperative that we move into positive, dream-enhancing environments so we don't struggle with the void created by leaving behind these harmful relationships or situations. We need to actively search out those environments that will help our dreams to flourish. Your dream may be to work for the United Nations helping the world's oppressed and marginalized. Why not start volunteering at an immigration center? Your desire may be to work with youth. So spend time with your church's youth group. By far the greatest environment to commit to is the local church.

It Hinges on the Local Church

It was hard to believe my little baby had set up house in my tummy. As she floated in her own little placental sac she was gaining all the nutrients she needed to grow and develop. For nine months my body was her entire world. In there she had everything she needed. The Church is to our potential what the womb is to a growing baby. Just as an embryo must implant itself in the wall of the uterus so it can grow, we too must implant ourselves in our local church in order to see our dreams become a reality. The local church feeds and nourishes our potential and dreams through a steady diet of praise and worship, Bible-based teaching, and relationships with people who will help keep us on track.

In my life I would not be who I am today if it wasn't for my local church. I believe being planted in a local church is a vital key to unearthing our potential. The Bible clearly shows us that those who are planted in God's house are promised a rich and abundant life.

> The [uncompromisingly] righteous shall flourish like the palm tree [be long-lived, stately, upright, useful and fruitful]; they shall grow like a cedar in Lebanon [majestic, stable, durable, and incorruptible]. Planted in the house of the Lord, they shall flourish in the courts of our God. [Growing in grace] they shall still bring forth fruit in old age; they shall be full of sap [of spiritual vitality] and [rich in the] verdure [of trust, love, and contentment]. *(Psalm 92:12-14)*

I was surprised when I first comprehended the significance of this Scripture and what it promised for my life. Growing up in the Greek Orthodox Church, I was never told that a relationship with Jesus and a healthy commitment to church could result in a life that was flourishing and successful. Maybe if someone had told me this at an earlier age I would have been more motivated to get out of bed on Sunday mornings. Instead I attended church as a religious ritual and obligation. The liturgy was two hours long (and in ancient Greek, which nobody understood) so I occupied this time by imagining what I had to do to get my picture on the wall along with all those other saints. When I found out I had to be martyred, I decided my picture in a photo album was good enough for me! Soon bored by church, I would pretend I was sound asleep when Mom came in to wake me up on Sundays. In time, she just gave up trying and church was relegated to something I did at Easter and Christmas (and not too willingly!).

Back then I couldn't fathom how Christianity could be relevant to anyone's daily life, or why anyone less than a hundred years old would ever want to go to church. That was until I encountered the house of God in a powerful and wonderful way. I walked into a church that was very differ-ent from the one I grew up in. What caught my attention was the fact that everyone looked genuinely happy to be there. There was singing, clapping (a no-no in my old church), and obvious joy in this place. I had never experi-enced anything like it. I have to admit I was a little freaked out, but something made me want to keep coming back week after week. (It was only later I realized the Holy Spirit had me cornered.)

It was in this environment that I discovered the differ-ence between a religious tradition and an authentic rela-tionship with a living Savior. As I planted myself in the house of God (note I said *planted*, not merely *attended*—

there's a big difference), I started to experience transformation in my life. The sermons contained life-giving, faith-filled Truths that revolutionized my thinking. Church also provided me with a safe place to process my feelings of fear, doubt, and frustration, and helped me understand why God had put me on the planet.

It was within the context of the local church that I found healing, hope, and the capacity to dream again. I found a loving community of people who accepted me unconditionally and helped me move beyond my past into the future God had for me. Now, it's through the Church that my destiny is being lived out.

The house of God should be a place where people can flourish, expand, and grow into all God has called them to be. It should be a place where dreams can be conceived, nurtured, and birthed. Admittedly, not all local churches provide this type of environment. I encourage you to seek out one that does.

I had no clue a church like mine existed in the whole world, much less just fifteen minutes away from my home. For the sake of our dreams we need to find the right church and decide to get planted. Only then will our roots go down deep and tap into all the promises of God.

※

Position

I don't know much about football but I do know that pre-game, during the game, and after the game, the coach pays a lot of attention to positioning. Our coach, God, is much the same. Before I understood the power of right position-ing I was taking steps to get myself into the right position (albeit, there were times the coach had to yell to get my at-tention!). I wanted to ensure when the ball (my dream, op-portunity, and responsibility) came my way all I had to do was run and score a touchdown. When it comes to being on the field remember:

1. Coach Put You on the Team

Life is a team sport and it's God who selected you for this exact time in history. He put you on the team with others—friends and peers (those people you're doing life with), men-tors (those people who challenge and inspire you), and disciples (those people you mentor)—knowing that you couldn't win the game alone.

➤ Don't leave the field—God doesn't want you to walk off the field the moment life doesn't seem to be going as you planned.

➤ Cling to your vision—It will help sustain you.

➤ Ask for help. We all need it. Use your teammates (your circle of friends and mentors) to encourage you.

➤ Spend time with the coach. Your relationship with God is the most important one. Depend on it like your life depends on it, because it does.

2. Coach Knows the Right Position for You

God positions us exactly where He wants us depending on what season of life we're in. There are times He puts us in an offensive position. This is when we start to see our dream gain momentum and experience breakthroughs and new opportunities. Other times we are playing on the defensive line—we may be facing an onslaught of opposition or challenge. In it all we need to hold fast to the fact that God positions us and He will never give us more than we can handle.

➤ Stay in position—God knows your strengths and your weaknesses, so don't go chasing things that haven't yet come your way.

➤ Don't try to take someone else's position—God wants you to live your life, not someone else's. Be obedient to all He has called you to be.

➤ Always be ready—You never know when the ball will come your way, so stay alert.

3. Coach Is Only a Time-Out Away

God is never far from the action. He is with us in the game, giving instructions, encouragement, and correction (particularly when we miss a pass). That's one of the great promises from the coach. He is always fully present—through the touchdowns and the fumbles. He will speak to you, stir your faith, and galvanize your dream.

➤ He is never too busy to chat—He is waiting to hear from you.

➤ His players (that's you) are His life—All you do and are interests Him.

➤ You need His direction—Listen for His voice.

Section 5

ENDURE

✼ Diary Entry

I want to know why they call it morning sickness when it lasts all day! It's a complete misnomer. Or maybe it's just because when you're flying over so many different time zones, it's bound to be morning somewhere down there!

I got on a United Airlines flight to L.A. today and I thought I was going to die. I was lying in my chair and I'm sure the flight attendant thought I had slipped into a coma. I was so tired, and the food . . . (Note to self: never say the word food again.)

How many more months of this do I have to endure? I'm sure the first day I don't feel like I've been hit by a bus will be the day I go into labor (and then I'll just look like a bus!). I hate to think what it's going to be like on a plane at eight *months' pregnant. I may have to buy two seats just so I can sit down.*

Nevertheless I press on. I am preaching twelve times in the next three days, and somehow I don't think doing it from bed is going to work.

There's Always a Process

I often wonder how my mother-in-law coped with being pregnant for almost ten years of her life (they obviously didn't have television), not to mention thirteen labors and thirteen sets of stretch marks. By my sixth month I wasn't even sure I was going to make it through just one pregnancy!

As eager as I was to meet my little girl and fast-track the process of pregnancy, I'm very glad God allowed nine months for Nick and I to prepare for our baby's arrival (I'm also very glad He didn't give us a twenty-two-month gestation period like elephants have). Due to our limited knowledge of all things baby, the forty weeks were as much for our benefit as they were for our little girl's.

This process was crucial. Like I said before, I made the most of this time by talking to parents, reading a plethora of books on successful parenting, and posing every imaginable question about pregnancy and motherhood to anyone who'd listen. (Part of my motivation was to try and discover if there was an alternative to labor—unfortunately, no.) It was imperative I endure the nine months of pregnancy, after all, I was going to be a mother for life. Likewise, there is a process we need to endure when it comes to birthing our dreams.

Far from being an unnecessary inconvenience, endurance is an essential ingredient in successfully realizing what God has put in our heart. It's through the process that we become the person we need to be to live out those dreams. Not to mention the process gives our unlocked potential time to grow and mature.

Often people try to bypass the process because it can appear difficult, long, and tedious. They opt instead for a shortcut to their dream. Just so you know, there are no shortcuts.

There's Always a Test

As difficult, uncomfortable, or even painful as enduring may be, the depth of the work we allow God to do *in us* during the process will ultimately determine how much He can do *through us.* (You may want to read that line again.)

In my life this reality was never more tested than when I decided to get serious about living for God and pursuing His purposes for my life. I was living for Jesus, actively involved in church and passionately pursuing my destiny. I wanted to go to the next level. It seemed that as soon as I made this decision God started bringing things to the surface that I didn't even know were there. I began hitting spiritual brick walls, and I felt like the more I wanted to grow, the less I was experiencing breakthrough. I suddenly found myself feeling angry, vulnerable, or irrationally self-conscious. Initially I attributed these emotions to my personality. I didn't realize these were symptoms of deeper issues. I would find myself withdrawing because I felt so extremely insecure. Yet I had this overwhelming need for approval, and I was driven by an unhealthy desire to succeed in every area of my life.

I know now that God wanted to clean me up from the inside out so I could achieve my destiny. I believe the reason He brought things to the surface at that point was because I was securely planted in my local church. God knew I had the support structures to help me deal with these issues because I was surrounded by people who were committed to my dreams.

Often it's when we make a decision to live for God and fulfill our dreams that the Holy Spirit starts to bring to the surface things hidden in our heart that could potentially sabotage our future. I was passionate for God and I wanted to move on, but Jesus was obviously trying to get my attention about something. I had to discover what that something was.

Around this time I attended a conference that related to my work at the youth center. I decided to go to a workshop on abuse because I had met many young people who had faced it in their own lives. I thought the workshop would give me some ideas about how I could help them. I hadn't had many opportunities to go to anything like this in the past, as the issue of abuse had only just come onto the public agenda. Prior to this, although people were aware that abuse happened, it was rarely discussed.

The speaker began to define abuse as something that causes harm or endangers a child's physical or psychological health and development through neglect or emotional, physical, or sexual mistreatment. She also talked about the consequences of being abused, and went on to say that people who experience abuse often downplay or deny its occurrence. The more she spoke the more I related to what she was saying. As I sat there I became suddenly aware of what God had been trying to bring to the surface in my own life. This woman was describing me!

I couldn't believe it. I ran out of the room sobbing uncontrollably. Someone had finally put into words what had happened to me as a young girl. I certainly didn't think of myself as abused, since so much of my life was great. I couldn't have asked for more amazing parents or brothers. Unfortunately, people they had trusted chose to violate that trust.

So deeply hidden was this part of my life that externally I seemed to have it all together. I was extremely successful at school and sports, and I had lots of friends. This, along with the fact there was no physical evidence of the abuse, meant that no one could have guessed what was going on.

Internally, years of suppressing, denying, and hiding finally caught up with me. That day at the workshop things I had forgotten and denied began to flood my mind. After so many years of trying to convince myself that what I experienced wasn't abuse, and mislabeling or downplaying the impact it had on my life, it suddenly became very clear to me. I kept hitting walls and having certain reactions because I had developed defense mechanisms to protect myself from ever being hurt again.

Finally, it all began to make sense. My fears, insecurities, response to authority, and need to be in control all stemmed from what happened to me as a child. I recognized I carried in my heart, deeply locked away, an underlying belief that God wasn't good. I wondered how a good God could possibly allow such bad things to happen to me. I saw God through the eyes of someone who had believed the promises made to her by people she trusted, only to be betrayed. It was shocking to realize this was all going on inside me. In order to be free it was essential I admit the truth of what had happened and allow God to begin the process of healing and restoration.

So began the journey. In the months following the conference I turned to God, desperate to overcome the pain, rejection, guilt, and shame I had been carrying for all those years. I read every book I could find on the subject. I started seeing a counselor. I consumed the Word of God and prayed like I'd never prayed before. I started to understand that even though my spirit was born again, my soul was scarred by the past. I needed healing. This wasn't an issue of salvation but of the quality of my life here on earth. To experience the abundant life God promised, and to unlock the potential that lay dormant in me, my wounded soul had to be healed. (God also knew that later in life I would discover that I was adopted, and I would have to settle the issues related to the abuse before I could tackle the issues surrounding my adoption.)

Again, it was the Truth contained in God's Word that was my anchor. In the Bible I read, "Beloved, I pray that you may prosper in every way and [that your body] may keep well, even as [I know] your soul keeps well and prospers" (3 John 1:2). Although I had read this Scripture literally hundreds of times it suddenly became real to me. God actually cared about every aspect of my life. He wanted me whole, but it was up to me to choose between staying bound by my past and embarking on the process of restoration. There really was no choice. If I was to experience all God had for me, I had to press on.

Press On

As hard as it often was (and I mean hard), I had to daily choose to keep pressing through the pain of my past and my fear of failure in order to have freedom. God wanted to give me a new identity as a whole and redeemed Christine. This didn't happen by simply responding to an altar call, where in an instant all that happened in my past disappeared. No, there was a process.

I first had to have a fresh revelation that Jesus had redeemed my life (and incidentally yours), and it was in and through Him that I was a new creation. I no longer had to be bound or held captive by the painful circumstances of my past.

> Therefore if any person is [ingrafted] in Christ (the Messiah) he is a new creation (a new creature altogether); the old [previous moral and spiritual condition] has passed away. Behold, the fresh and new has come! *(2 Corinthians 5:17)*

It was the Truth of this Scripture that gave me the power to allow the Holy Spirit, the ultimate Healer of our soul, to enter the deep areas of my wounded heart. As painful as the memories were, it was essential that I let God into these broken places. During this phase of the process the Holy Spirit pinpointed areas in me that were damaged. He also began to reveal the action I needed to take to live a life beyond my past.

One of the biggest areas was my subconscious belief that the only person I could trust was me. The reason for this belief was that my trust had been violated through the abuse. In order to protect myself I began to live in a way that ensured I was always in control. I tried to maintain control of my thoughts, my circumstances, and often the people around me (this was an exhausting way to live). This posed a few problems, particularly because God wanted me to hand over control of my life to Him. He held the keys to my destiny, but as long as I was sitting in the driver's seat it was impossible for Him to direct my life.

A vital step in the healing process was admitting I couldn't control everything (not from a lack of trying!). I had to consciously allow God to start steering my life. This sounds a lot easier than it actually was. It took sheer faith to put my trust in God, but once I did I began to appreciate just how incredible the adventure with Him really is.

Forgiving

Forgiving those who had abused me was possibly the most difficult part of my journey to wholeness. It took all the courage and endurance I could muster because it meant I had to walk through parts of my past I would have much preferred to forget. The one thing worse, however, than being abused would be to carry the perpetrators of that abuse in my heart forever through unforgiveness and bitterness. The only way I would experience complete healing was through forgiveness.

Nothing in me wanted to forgive my abusers because I didn't think they deserved it. But deep down I knew unforgiveness had hardened my heart, and if unresolved, would jeopardize my future. I went to the Word of God for strength. The words of Matthew 6:14-15 helped me move in the direction of forgiveness.

> For if you forgive people their trespasses [their reckless and willful sins, leaving them, letting them go, and giving up resentment], your heavenly Father will also forgive you. But if you do not forgive others their trespasses . . . neither will your Father forgive you your trespasses.

This Scripture makes it abundantly clear we have no right to withhold forgiveness. It's not an issue of whether the abusers deserved my forgiveness or not. It all comes back to Jesus. He forgave us for the debt we owed Him. Therefore we have no other choice but to forgive others for the debt they owe us.

As hard as it was, it was this Truth I had to reconcile in my heart. Only then would I be ready to forgive. The right time came one night during a prayer counseling session. After what seemed like hours the counselor said, "Christine, now it's your turn. You have to forgive." I fell to my knees sobbing and stayed there for hours, unable to articulate the simple words, "I forgive them." I was full of pain, anger, and bitterness. Even though I knew the only way I'd be free was to forgive, I didn't want to. I felt that if I did, somehow it would mean that what happened to me was okay.

It was there on the floor that night that something finally broke in me. Although I never would forget I was abused, at that moment my past no longer had power over my future. The blood of Jesus does not cause amnesia; it provides a life beyond the past. That evening I was finally able to say those words of forgiveness. The instant they left my mouth I experienced a deep sense of release from the burden I had been carrying for twenty years.

Forgiveness that night was granted to more than just those who abused me. I also had to forgive myself for carrying the internal bruising of my past for so many years. I had lived my life carrying the shame and guilt of my past. I had to hand this all over to God as well. This too was a daily decision as the emotions associated with my abuse didn't immediately disappear as soon as I had forgiven. Walking in forgiveness is a daily choice.

For you to be all God says you can be, you will have to address the bitterness and unforgiveness that may have taken root in your heart. You may need to forgive a parent for the negative words or criticism they spoke over you, a spouse who walked out on you, a friend who rejected or hurt you, or an employer who wronged you. Like me, you may also need to forgive yourself for holding onto the pain, the bitterness, the hate, or the anger these situations may have caused. The power of forgiveness will set you free. Forgiving others and myself brought incredible freedom to my life—spiritually, physically, and emotionally. This in turn paved the way for me to trust again.

It Takes Trust

Trusting God was one thing, but my past had also caused me to mistrust people. This had a detrimental effect on my ability to build relationships, and not surprisingly, on my social life! As a result, I was extremely lonely despite the fact I was constantly surrounded by people. My life was proof that you can be in a crowd, but internally be totally disconnected.

During this time the Holy Spirit began to break down the walls I had built around my heart in an effort to stop others from getting close to me. It soon became clear to me that God has a sense of irony. He used people—as scary as they were—to rebuild my trust in people.

It started one Wednesday afternoon in my local sandwich shop. I had gone in to buy the ultimate carb fix (mandatory fries and potato scallops topped with ketchup), and there standing at the counter was Kylie. She was the thin (waiflike actually) blonde woman ordering a salad sandwich on whole-grain bread—"hold the butter please." I recognized Kylie from church and began to chat with her. This was the beginning of a friendship God used to powerfully restore me.

I was passionate about working with young people (and my chips and scallops), while her passion was the gym. We made a deal. I would go to the gym as long as Kylie volunteered at the youth center. I thought I was doing my God duty by helping her become more spiritual, while all along God was using her to rebuild my shattered self-image. I can't recount the times she walked through the valleys and endured the process with me. She helped me see things as they really were, not as I saw them. She accepted me despite my shortcomings and insecurities, and she believed in me even when I didn't. She kept me focused on my dream and wouldn't let me give up.

It wasn't just friendships that were negatively affected by my past. My ability to form intimate relationships had also been impacted. This is where Nick came into the picture. God brought him into my life to help me overcome my fear of intimacy (just one of the reasons he came into my life). As much as I tried to push Nick away and suppress how I felt about him (remember the walls?), he continued loving me.

One night I was again attempting to convince him why we should break up. After going through my twenty points, I looked up at him and said, "So what do you think?" The expression on his face said it all. "Christine, I don't know what is going on inside you, and I have no real response to your barrage of reasons, but all I can say is that God has told me to love you unconditionally and to love you back to wholeness."

I sat there dumbfounded. He had totally undone every one of my arguments and doubts with that simple, yet profound response. No one had ever said anything like that to me before. I knew then that Nick was the man with whom I was going to spend the rest of my life. Nick had the tenacity to persist even when all others would have thrown their hands up in despair! He has been there every step of the way, and our relationship is stronger now than ever. (Have I mentioned he's a babe?)

Learning to trust people started with me allowing the someones God brought across my path to get close enough to help walk me through the process and into my future.

Learning to trust God, allowing the Holy Spirit to do a deep work, and the power of forgiveness were all part of the process of restoration. There were times I wished I could shortcut the process, but the damage to my soul was caused over many years. Instant restoration, although not impossible for God, was not likely. This fact wasn't always easy to accept. There were many times that everything in my flesh wanted to run from the process, but my spirit wanted to push through to the freedom I knew was mine on the other side of my obedience.

It was in the testing of my obedience that God was building my character. He allowed me to be confronted by circumstances that helped develop love, patience, joy, peace, kindness, long-suffering (very long), and self-control. These were all qualities I would need in the future God had waiting for me.

As I began to discover the awesome benefits of pursuing God, it became easier to resist my fleshly desires and harder to stay in the pit of self-pity, negativity, and fear. Obedience wasn't so much about giving up something good, but rather chasing something better. I wanted more of Jesus in my life and I was ready to endure anything to have it. As challenging, uncomfortable, and frightening as it sometimes was, the person I am now is a direct result of my choice to endure the process.

I realized just how far I'd come during a beautiful dinner

with Nick. We'd just gotten engaged and were discussing the exciting future that lay ahead of us. He took my hand in his across the table and looked deep into my eyes. "Honey, do you know what my greatest goal in life is?" he asked. I was waiting for a romantic monologue expressing his complete love and devotion, so I was momentarily stunned when instead he said, "One day I want to be able to love you almost as much as you do."

I began to laugh hysterically. Never one to be short for words, I answered, "Well, babe, it's in your best interest that I love myself this much." He looked at me in amazement and asked, "Why?"

"What's the greatest commandment in the Bible?" I asked.

He cautiously responded, "To love the Lord our God with all of our heart, mind, and strength."

"And what else?"

"To love your neighbor as yourself," he added.

"That's exactly right," I said. "And that's the problem with most of humanity. We do love our neighbor just as we love ourselves; it's just that we don't really like ourselves."

Nick's romantic comment was the ultimate compliment. With all I had faced in life I didn't think I would ever be able to love myself this way. I could have chosen to give up on the process, but if I had, I never would have reached this point. This was the fruit of obedience. Joyce Meyer often says, "Hurting people hurt people." While I was hurting, my life and ministry flowed from a place of brokenness. It was only when I allowed God to heal and restore me that I could serve people from a place of strength and wholeness. This only happened because I chose to endure.

When it comes to enduring, we need to take the advice of the former prime minister of Britain, Winston Churchill. In 1941, as Europe was being torn apart by World War II, he made this speech to students at the Harrow School:

> Never give in. Never give in. Never, never, never, never—in nothing, great or small, large or petty—never give in, except to convictions of honor and good sense. Never yield to force. Never yield to the apparently overwhelming might of the enemy.[iii]

Never give up.

§

Endure

Right now you're probably reeling from my latest disclosure. Writing about my abuse was one of the most difficult things I have ever done. But I know my story will help forge in your heart the Truth that, regardless of what you've been through (or are currently facing), endurance isn't an option. It's fundamental to birthing your dream. Reading my testimony and enduring your own life are two very different things. I hope these practical steps will help make it a reality.

1. Never Say Die—To Your Dream

Undoubtedly if the fire you're facing is hot enough there will come a point where you will feel like lying down and never getting up. Through the worst of it, for me, this was every other hour! When you feel like you've been hit by a steamroller make sure you:

➤ Get out of bed.
➤ Decide to endure.

- Stand on the Word of God.
- Look for the positive—Is the sun still shining?
- Keep praising God.
- Forgive those people that may have hurt you.
- Remember God's refining you through the furnace.

2. Never Forget—God Is God

Nothing is too big for God. Whatever you're up against He is still in control. When we are facing tough times, the temptation is to start believing that God has forsaken us. Even when you think He has moved to Antarctica, He truly is fighting right alongside you. Meditate on these truths as often as you need to:

- God is Faithful.
- His provision is constant.
- He has a purpose for you.
- He loves you.

3. Never Underestimate—The Power of the Test

Great teaching and leadership is awesome, but the thing that impacts people the most is someone's testimony. It's easy to argue theology or semantics but it's tough disputing someone's personal experience. Our biggest test will be our greatest testimony to others if we choose to endure it. Think about it. This book shares some of my most difficult times. But by sharing my trials I want to encourage you to recognize all that God has called you to be. Remember:

➤ The test isn't all about you—God will use your story to transform lives.
➤ You don't have to be fully through it before you start sharing your testimony.
➤ Remember Jesus—His greatest test became the world's greatest gift.

Section 6

ENLARGE

✿ Diary Entry

I was standing in an elevator today and a perfect stranger came and touched my tummy. No one ever tried doing that to me before I was pregnant! There seems to be a universal magnet that draws people to me. For some reason they feel that touching my stomach while they speak to me is comforting (for them maybe!).

I'm feeling rather whale-like actually. I had to go on a bit of a shopping expedition, as my clothes are getting a little snug (the button popped off my favorite shirt, but I'm sure it was already loose). What I discovered is that nice maternity wear doesn't exist. I so don't want to look like a tent on legs! I have never been so excited about elastic and fabrics that have a little give. It's a whole new world.

And what's with the labor stories? I think I have now heard every conceivable delivery story: women who have delivered in their car, on the side of the road, or on the bathroom floor . . . and they're not even the horror stories! Do people really believe that reliving someone else's labor in graphic detail is helping put my mind at ease? Well it's not! (Note to self: get rid of sign on forehead that says, "Come tell me your traumatic birthing story.") No more please! I have resolved to put my hands over my ears and hum a happy tune anytime I see a woman pushing a stroller, in an attempt to deter her from mentioning labor.

Our Capacity

Just like that, I could no longer fit into anything in my wardrobe (actually I felt like a wardrobe!). How did that happen? Had the baby bypassed the umbilical cord and tapped directly into my stomach for her food supply? I always wondered how a woman's stomach could stretch enough to carry a baby, and there it was, happening right before my very eyes. Where did all that extra skin come from? Did I have that much excess lying around?

My dream of having a baby had now totally invaded my personal space. What started as something unobtrusive (except to my eating habits) had now grown to the point it defined how I looked, what I wore, how I acted, and the things I spoke about (I couldn't remember the last time I had a non-baby-related conversation). I had to accept that I could no longer carry the baby that was growing inside of me and stay the same size.

My stomach was stretching at a rapid pace. I saw my belly button from an angle I didn't know existed, and I was sure my baby thought my bladder was either a trampoline or a pillow, depending on what time of day it was. People no longer had to try and guess if I was really pregnant or if I had simply eaten too much chocolate cake and gained a few pounds. It was out there for all to see, friend and stranger alike. I was having a baby!

During this phase of my pregnancy I would wake up each morning wondering what would be different that day. Anything was possible. First a placenta appeared from nowhere to feed the baby inside me (I hoped she liked garlic) and then I became the human equivalent of a dairy cow. There was nothing I could do to stop this process of change and enlargement (nor did I want to); ultimately the more I expanded, the healthier and better developed my baby would be.

Enlargement is also necessary in birthing our dreams. God needs us to become big people (and I'm not referring to your waistline) because the larger we are, the more He can entrust to us. Our role in the enlargement process is pivotal. We must proactively pursue those things that will help us become all God intends us to be.

Many of us are praying for God to supernaturally enlarge us, when He is in fact waiting for us to grow to where we need to go. This concept is powerfully exemplified to us in the Parable of the Talents (Mathew 25:14-30). In this parable, a master is preparing to leave on a long journey (on camels, every trip is long). Before he leaves, he gives three of his servants talents (resources) and responsibilities based on their level of ability. In today's terms, this would be like a boss giving his employees resources and authority to run the office while he went away on a business trip. This is exactly what God does with us. He gives us resources—gifts, abilities, anointing, favor, opportunity, and provision—every day based on our level of enlargement.

In the parable, what the servants did with what they were given was crucial. Two of the servants utilized, multiplied, and increased their resources. The third servant chose to dig a hole and bury his. When the master finally returned from his trip, he called the servants together to find out what they did while he was away. To the two who had multiplied their talents he said,

> Well done, you upright (honorable, admirable) and faithful servant! You have been faithful and trustworthy over a little; I will put you in charge of much. Enter into and share the joy (the delight, the blessedness) which your master enjoys. *(Matthew 25:21)*

But to the servant who buried his talent he said, "You wicked and lazy and idle servant!" (v. 26). The master then took back what he'd given to him, leaving the servant with nothing.

I used to think this was a pretty harsh response from the master. After all, the servant kept his talent safe and took good care of it. But what I realized from this is God doesn't want us to simply maintain what we've been given. He's expecting us to grow and multiply it. If we're faithful with everything He has put in our hands right now, our lives will be fruitful.

Our faithfulness, or good stewardship, will also influence how much more God can pour into our lives. God's resources are unlimited. It's not our skill levels, past experiences, or gender which limit how much He will pour in. Nor is it our culture, tradition, or socioeconomic background that will determine how much we receive (unless we let them). The key to unleashing all God has for us is doing something (digging a hole doesn't count) with what God has already put in our hands.

Where we are now may seem a long way from where we want to be. You could be a waitress who wants to be a movie star, a college student who wants to be a doctor, or a church usher who really wants to be a preacher. The size of what we start with doesn't matter. Everything has the potential to grow and multiply. Regardless of where we are in life right now, we need to ensure we're being good stewards over what we've been given. As we enlarge and our capacity grows, so too will our opportunities and influence. On the other hand, if we're currently mismanaging, ignoring, or belittling what God has already given us, why would He entrust us with more to mismanage, ignore, and belittle? The key is to stay faithful and committed, and in time God will give us more. This principle applies to every area of our life—spiritual, emotional, relational, financial, and physical.

This has certainly been proven in my own life. When I was asked to run a Bible study for a few young girls from church I was excited by the opportunity to help them grow in their relationship with God and with each other. I was no Bible scholar, but I was determined to make Tuesdays the best night of their week. For me, it was more than just meeting once a week. I was committed to doing life with these girls.

I picked them up in my beat-up car (which I even tried to clean) and I drove them to church so they could hear the Word and get connected to the house of God. I took them out for coffee so I could get to know them better and find out about their dreams. I prayed for them, encouraged them, and believed in them. I even prepared for hours before we met each week to ensure the half-hour discussion was God-inspired (and to ensure I actually had a clue what I was going to say). These girls began to flourish, and it didn't take long until the group grew so large that we couldn't all be in the same room at the same time! I simply did something with what I'd been given so God could entrust me with more.

There came a time when our church decided it really wanted a youth outreach to the community in the form of a youth center. I was asked to be a part of the founding team, and I applied the same principles (and enthusiasm) there as I did with my group of girls. We saw the center as an opportunity to impact the lives of the young people in our city. With this is mind we developed new community-based initiatives, secured funding to run programs that would give people a future and a hope, and started a youth newspaper that provided a real (and relevant) voice for youth. We invaded high schools and universities with a message of purpose and destiny. It was there I developed the capacity and skills that allowed me to move into the next phase of my journey.

When I was promoted to be the director of our state's youth movement, all I had learned at the youth center aided me with my new responsibilities. I did all I knew to do, as I saw this as an opportunity to mobilize and influence a generation of young people. We worked interdenominationally to help unite youth ministries, and held large-scale evangelistic youth events in stadiums all across our state. It was because I increased my personal capacity that I went from filling school auditoriums to filling stadiums. Thank God I learned to speak to an audience of five hundred when I had the chance, because I now found myself speaking to ten thousand people at a time! I simply did something with what I'd been given, so God could entrust me with more.

Without a doubt, I know if I hadn't been faithful with

the opportunities and resources God put in my hand during those years, my personal capacity would never have been enlarged and stretched enough to do what I'm doing today. Together with Nick I now travel all over the world, preaching, teaching, and helping to build God's Church. I've literally spoken to hundreds of thousands of people and had the privilege of seeing tens of thousands come to Christ. I'm now living the dream I had in my heart all those years ago, but it started with that small group of girls (and my beat-up car).

Bust Off the Limitations

If we're truly serious about increasing our personal capacity, we need to address the limitations that could be an obstacle to our enlargement. We all have limitations. Some that we can do something about, others that we can do absolutely nothing about.

Take my singing for example (if you can call it that). As anointed as it sounds in the shower, I'm confident I will never lead public worship—ever! Although I passionately love to worship God, I'm called to be a preacher not a song leader. I don't have the potential in me to be an effective worship leader because that's not what God put me on earth to do. If I spent all my time frustrated, praying, and fasting for doors of opportunity to open in the area of music ministry, I would miss reaching all the people I'm called to reach. Besides, my singing voice would prevent multitudes from ever entering into true worship!

The tragedy is that so many people do exactly this. They spend all their time trying to pray away the limitations they can do nothing about, and in the process they completely miss God's plan for their lives. Our energy would be better spent trying to eliminate those things we can actually do something about. These are the limitations that are generally self-imposed. You know the ones we try to find excuses for? Our unrealized potential lies in de-limiting these limitations.

If your dream is to win a gold medal at the Olympic games, then you need to have a coach (preferably one in your chosen discipline) and train daily. If your dream is to be a doctor, you'll need to get a degree (preferably one in medicine). If you want to be a chef, you'll need to be a little more adventurous in the kitchen than making instant noodles every night.

De-limiting the limitations we can will take change. Where and who we are today is the sum total of the choices we've made to this point. If we want to be somewhere different in one year, five years, or ten years, we need to be willing to implement emotional, spiritual, intellectual, and physical changes in our lives. The fact is, without change nothing changes.

I discovered this to be true when Nick and I decided we wanted to have a baby. I was thirty-four and my commitment to exercise had severely diminished since my gym-going days with Kylie. My love of carbohydrates on the other hand had only increased (my Greek love of pasta). My definition of exercise was now the sixty-foot walk from my front door to the car.

Overall I didn't feel good and my energy levels were depleted. I could not blame my busy lifestyle for this, nor could I attribute it to fashion designers putting the wrong size on my clothes (although I did try this excuse on several occasions). I had some forewarning from friends that this lethargy would only get worse with a baby in the equation, so I decided my health could no longer be a limitation in my life. This wasn't motivated by vanity; I just did not want my daughter's preschool friends to think I was her grandmother! This meant change. I had to adjust what I ate, increase my level of activity, and make some lifestyle choices to ensure I would have the future with my daughter I envisioned.

Enlarging spiritually in my case meant shrinking physically. It wasn't always comfortable (let me tell you!), but if I had resisted change and spiritual enlargement, I would have ended up living the very future I didn't want to have.

Settling for what is comfortable is one of the biggest enemies to our enlargement. Life can become very repetitive, and those things we've grown accustomed to—the nice lifestyle, hours spent watching the television night after night, or sleeping in on a Sunday morning (and missing church), can make us resistant to change.

In every season of life—whether we're married, single, buying a house, starting a new career, going to college, or starting a family—we need to be committed to enlarging our personal capacity (even when it's not comfortable). We need to refuse to be satisfied with our latest accomplishments, as what we've accomplished is no longer our potential because it has been actualized. There's always potential within us waiting to be tapped.

I'm not suggesting we can do whatever we want to do, be whatever we want to be, or have whatever we want to have. But I do believe if our desires are God's desires, and our dreams are God-given, then He has equipped us with the ability to increase our capacity to see these dreams achieved. To successfully birth our dreams we must be committed to growing where we need to go.

Walk It Out

ॐ

Enlarge

Whether it's in pregnancy or with our dreams, enlargement has a purpose—to help us carry more. Here are some practical tips I have used in my life to help me enlarge spiritually (no tips for belly enlargement necessary—our bodies have that all worked out).

1. Do Something You've Never Done Before

I read an article many years ago about an order of French nuns whose average age was ninety. The journalist asked them for the secret to their longevity. Their response was twofold: a commitment to keep their minds active by continually reading and learning, and every month they did something they had never done before. If it works for ninety-year-old nuns (by that age, you would expect they would begin to run out of new things to do!) it will work for you. Why not:

➤ Research the Web or read a book about a subject you know absolutely nothing about?

➤ Pay for the toll of the car behind you when passing through the tollgate.

➤ Pick up the lunch tab for the people at the table next to you.

➤ Learn a new language.

➤ Enroll in a college or night class in something you've always been interested in but never thought was very practical.

➤ Develop a new skill (basket weaving?).

2. Go Where You've Never Been

I've always dreamed of living a life of influence and therefore look for opportunities to stretch me (even if they're not always convenient). I have traveled to nations where children go hungry and the people are oppressed because not only do I bring a message of hope—Jesus—but because these experiences will enlarge and challenge me. Get out of your comfort zone!

➤ Visit a retirement home and spend time with the elderly.

➤ Go to the rough part of your town (with company of course) to see how others live and how you can help.

➤ Go to an art gallery or museum.

➤ Get involved with a charity that feeds the homeless.

➤ Volunteer at a youth crisis center.

3. Speak To Someone You've Never Spoken To

It's funny how we can charge through life, never really noticing the people that we cross paths with. A few years ago, in a rush to get home, I barely said hello to the cashier at my local store. Then came the prompting of the Holy Spirit. This young woman was in the midst of a crisis and needed someone to speak to. After her shift was over we talked for two hours. I could have completely missed this God opportunity because I was too busy to stop and speak to someone. Why not say something to:

> The person sitting next to you on the bus or train (especially if it's someone you know!).
> The guy lifting weights next to you at the gym.
> The woman standing next to you in the elevator.
> The cashier at the grocery store.
> The person that comes to your door trying to sell you something.

Section 7

PREPARE

✺ Diary Entry

*N*ick *and I went to our first childbirth class tonight.*
It was all a little too graphic for Nick. He didn't fare so well.
The midwife was stretching a knitted tube (which was supposed
to represent the uterus) over the head of a plastic doll to demon-
strate the level of expansion my uterus would need to go through
(lots) if I was going to have any hope of delivering the baby suc-
cessfully. I heard a deep breath and I turned to see an extremely
pale and clammy Nick. He couldn't bear the thought of it. I was
so embarrassed because I thought he was going to pass out. I put
up my hand on Nick's behalf (he didn't have the strength) to get
permission for him to go to the bathroom.

All my classmates were a little perplexed at why he never
made it back to class. I discovered at the end of the night that

he spent his first trip to the hospital in the waiting room (and this wasn't even the labor!). From now on, Mom or Pastor Bobbie will be coming to the classes with me. I just don't think Nick will survive (and I want my daughter to meet her father).

The classes are supposed to prepare me for the real thing. I think I would rather it be a surprise. Everyone keeps telling me I need to be educated and trained by someone who has gone to the labor ward and lived to tell about it. I don't know how much good it will do. Due to another dreaded side effect of pregnancy, I now have the memory of a goldfish (about twenty seconds duration). I'm sure that by the time I have finished classes the only thing I will remember in any detail is the knitted uterus demonstration. I hope the rest of it will come back to me during the labor.

The other totally bizarre thing is my unnatural urge to nest and get things ready. (I've even cooked a few meals!) We're in the process of moving to be closer to Mom's place so the baby can have a great relationship with Grandma (and I'll have a babysitter on call). The baby's room is all set up and I've bought every item a baby could ever need (actually multiples of each— I don't think twenty-two onesies is unreasonable).

All the while I'm carrying the equivalent of a watermelon around my waist. Pretty impressive, huh?

Are You Ready?

I couldn't walk past a newsstand without buying every home or garden magazine available. Seemingly overnight the spirit of nesting came upon me, and all the documentaries I had ever watched about birds making nests took on new meaning.

I've never been one to hoard much of anything. In fact, Nick and our team are very careful not to leave anything important anywhere I might get my hands on it, as inevitably it will end up being filed—in the garbage can. So nesting was extremely unusual for me. All my friends who had children assured me that, just like birds, nesting was instinctive for mothers-to-be. Relieved, I put my hormone-induced zeal to good use for anything relating to baby.

With the aid of my to-do list (the original list having been reworked forty-seven times), I began to accumulate everything one could possibly need or want for baby: clothes, furniture, toys, and dozens of onesies and socks. I wanted to ensure I was ready for our little girl's arrival.

Like birthing a baby, preparation is vital in birthing our dreams. There are certain preparations that can only be made immediately prior to our dream being birthed. For Nick and I, the preparation included childbirth classes (but I, unlike Nick, made it through the entire six weeks). They helped prepare me for the reality of giving birth, and sealed the fact that I definitely wanted to skip the labor!

The delivery date was drawing closer and no one but God really knew when our little girl would be ready to come out. We had to be prepared for all possible scenarios. We had the overnight bag packed in the car (yes, complete with new pajamas, item thirty-one on my original to-do list), we had several routes to the hospital mapped out and timed, and Nick had every possible emergency number programmed into his cell phone—including the fire department. You really can never be too prepared.

Preparation always precedes something new. It's pivotal that we be prepared if we want to successfully birth the dreams God has put in our hearts. It could be going back to school, learning new skills, securing a loan, or saving for that missions trip.

Imagine if I had waited until after our baby was born to prepare for her arrival. Not only would she have nothing to wear home from the hospital (!), we would have had to spend time solving the problems caused by our lack of preparation when we should have been enjoying the realization of our dream—our little girl.

Our level of preparation reveals to God (and others) our

level of expectancy. If we're not willing to do what's necessary to ensure we can birth our dream, we really have to question just how seriously we want it.

Make Room

As the birth of our baby quickly approached, Nick and I had to make some tough decisions. Although we loved living in the city, and especially being within walking distance of some of Sydney's best cafes, we lived forty-five minutes from my mom's house and from church. I knew I would need my mom more than my lattes once the baby arrived, so in preparation, we decided to move.

Moving was not only important in order for me to have all the support systems I would need as a new mom, it also gave Nick and I an opportunity to do one final sweep of all the clutter we had (actually Nick had) accumulated. We needed to physically make room for our baby.

We also need to be willing to make room in our lives for the impending birth of our dreams. This might mean emptying our life of clutter such as wasted time, energy, resources, or draining relationships. These things can jeopardize our dreams by distracting us at a time when we should be more focused than ever.

Sometimes we think it's only negative or ungodly things we have to clean up or remove in order to realize our dreams. Often times, though, particularly the further along in the Christian journey we are, we have to let go of things that may be good for the season we're currently in, but may not be good for the next phase of our journey. For example, I used to play squash every Thursday night (there's nothing like hitting a little black ball around to help relieve stress). But when our church leadership night was changed to Thursdays, I chose to give up the competition. Why? I knew that serving in church and growing as a leader, not squash, was going to take me to my dreams.

Even now Nick and I have to continually make concessions. We travel most of the year, so it's not always easy to do some of the things we used to do. We cannot always see our friends as often as we'd like (thank God for e-mail), and sometimes we have to miss a Greek wedding or two.

In our own life, we may dream of going to Africa as a missionary. To make room for this dream we'll have to give up aspects of the life we currently know (maybe even our hairdryer). Our dream may be a job promotion, but with it we may have to let go of a work project we initiated and developed. If we're not willing to let these things go, as good as they are, they can become an anchor or weight that keeps us out of the future God has for us.

Expect the Unexpected

My expected date of delivery was March 2, 2002. I was really excited because I knew I was going to have a four-hour labor and that I would be out of hospital the very same day (I was dreaming!). This would give me ten days to master the finer points of motherhood and still make it to our church's annual women's conference where I could show off my baby girl to thousands of my closest friends.

Well our little girl had other plans. As the due day came and went there was still no sign of her. I grew desperate and began trying every home remedy in existence in an attempt to induce labor. I drank castor oil, had my pressure points massaged, tried jumping up and down a hundred times, ran (oh, what a sight that was), and put my feet in extremely hot water—all to no avail. The fact was that no amount of planning or praying on my part was going to cause my baby to come any sooner than she was supposed to. Our little girl obviously had a revelation about God's timing. She clearly was familiar with Ecclesiastes 3:1 which says, "To everything there is a season, and a time for every matter or purpose under heaven." She wasn't budging.

When it comes to our dreams, we can prepare, plan, and try to twist God's arm in an attempt to accelerate the birth. We can often think we are somehow helping God by trying to force open doors only He can open. We may want to get married or experience financial breakthrough or get that promotion. But rather than trusting that God has it under control we try to make our dreams happen by running ahead of Him. Like I did, we try to take matters into our own hands. The result is that it may cause us to give birth to our dreams prematurely.

I remember seeing the effects of premature birth during a visit to the intensive care nursery. In the incubators lay tiny little babies who had been born preterm (before the thirty-seven-week mark). Many of them had tubes in their noses to assist their breathing and machines that were monitoring their heartbeat. Depending on how premature they were the consequences could be anything from being slightly underweight to disability or death.

In relation to dreams, giving birth prematurely can also have debilitating effects. It may cause us to birth a dream that is so underdeveloped that the first sign of attack, criticism, setback, or disappointment is enough to destroy it. In the worst cases our dreams may be stillborn. By trying to accelerate the birth we're effectively putting our dreams at risk.

As we approach the labor ward we need to be prepared to go the distance and allow God to take us to full term. It is God who brings our dreams to pass in His perfect, divine timing. (So chill out. If it's God, it will happen.)

Prepare

People can get so caught up in the fact their dream is so close—preparing here, there, and everywhere—but forget they still have to finish this season before launching into the next one. I have had lots of opportunities to finish things—jobs, relationships, renovating my house (!). The most important lesson I've gained from all of this is the way we finish one thing directly impacts the way we enter the new thing.

1. Don't Devalue the Season You're In

The reason you have not given birth yet is that God obviously has more for you to learn in the season you are currently in. Maybe it's a lesson in relationships, money management, or cleanliness. (Want an office with a view? Try keeping your current work space tidy.) Regardless of the subject matter, these lessons help prepare you for the labor ward and beyond. Don't forget to:

➤ Recognize and reflect on how far this present season has brought you.

➤ Ask the question: Is there more to learn here?

➤ Appreciate the opportunities this season has given you.

2. Don't Drop the Ball

You may be on the brink of giving birth to a new dream, but that's no excuse for forgetting your current responsibilities. That would be like someone who was getting a departmental promotion in six months deciding to take a four-day weekend every week. Only you can decide what kind of legacy and example you want to leave. A positive finish might involve:

➤ Training new leaders.

➤ Getting the accounts up-to-date.

➤ Developing new systems or writing a how-to manual.

➤ Teaching someone the ropes.

➤ Working ahead of schedule to make the transition smoother once you're gone.

➤ Leaving the tape dispenser and stapler behind.

3. Don't Burn Your Bridges

Entering a new phase doesn't necessarily mean cutting out everyone and everything from the season you're leaving. While people in your current season might not be coming into the next phase of your journey, they may very well play a part in your future.

➤ Don't gloat over the fact that you're moving on and maybe others are not.
➤ Always value people for the part they've played in your life (however small that may be).
➤ Say thank you—maybe even buy chocolates to show your appreciation!

Section 8

LABOR

✿ Diary Entry

Date: March 9, 2002

1:32 P.M.: *W*hat was that? Did my water just break? I'm
sure this generally involves water, but I call Mom just in case.
She comes over and assures me I would know if my water had
in fact broken, as would whatever surface I was sitting on at the
time (note to self: don't sit down).

I have been feeling little contractions all day but everyone
keeps telling me I'm just trying to will the baby to come so I
don't miss the women's conference (it starts in two days!). I'm in-
sulted by their comments (maybe some of it's true), but I know
something feels different.

4:48 P.M.: Okay, now who's laughing? All evidence is pointing to the baby wanting out! My contractions are six and a half minutes apart (give or take a few seconds), and let me tell you, Braxton Hicks is nowhere in sight! I decide a faith-filled environment is the best place to be in my condition, so Nick and I are heading to Saturday night church. I'm sitting on a plastic bag just in case.

5:38 P.M.: Arrive at church.

5:40 P.M.: Finally get out of the car. (Thank God Nick notices the plastic bag stuck to my legs.)

5:41 P.M.: Waddle through the foyer.

5:46 P.M.: I make it up the stairs. All my friends are here at church tonight as they're in town for the women's conference. They're all praying I'll have the baby while they're still in the country. By the feel of things, I think God has heard their prayers.

6:38 P.M.: Here we go again! Contractions are now four and a half minutes apart. I have no idea what the message is. I'm finding it a little difficult to concentrate as I try (as inconspicuously as possible) to time my contractions (note to self: must keep pained look off my face so I won't distract Pastor Brian).

7:44 P.M.: Everyone is having a bite to eat after the service, except the huddle of women around me who are helping time my contractions. Di has come prepared with a stopwatch. Like clockwork—three minutes apart.

8:23 P.M.: Di, who has twin boys and a four-year-old girl, suggests we call the hospital. Thinking she should know, Nick obliges. The friendly nurse suggests we make our way to the hospital.

8:36 P.M.: A small entourage prepares to leave the church with Nick and me (and baby of course) to provide some moral support and comic relief between each contraction. There's another one!

8:52 P.M.: I'm sitting on my plastic bag again but I seriously think this is going to be a false alarm. We'll get to the hospital, they'll take one look at me, and off to home we'll go. Alternatively I will be admitted, I'll have the baby in four hours and be back in church in the morning.

10:00 P.M.: Guess we won't be going home yet (not one of the seven of us). I've been admitted and I'm 0.5 centimeters dilated. Now what did they say in the childbirth class about dilation? Remember, Chris, remember. So much for it all coming back to me in the labor ward; I'm here, but my memory hasn't shown up yet!

10:03 P.M.: I ask the nurse about rate of dilation. Okay, I'm supposed to dilate three centimeters per hour. So by 1:30 A.M., at the latest, it should all be over and I will still get a good night's rest.

10:36 P.M.: So far so good. I have no idea what all the mothers of the world complain about. Contractions aren't that painful. Uncomfortable maybe.

10:38 P.M.: I express my delight about how easy it is to Di and Maree. Amused, they try to convince me I have no idea of what's about to hit me.

10:49 P.M.: Ooouchh . . . how right they were!!!

No Pain No Gain

I can't clearly remember what happened next, but Di says it wasn't a pretty sight. I deny everything! I had been admitted to the hospital at 10:00 P.M. By 2:00 A.M. everyone except Nick, Maree, and Di had left. At that point I was excited to see the midwife, since I was sure I had dilated at least seven centimeters. This meant the baby would be arriving anytime now.

After a thorough examination she uttered the words no woman in my condition ever wants to hear, "Nothing's changed." The blood drained from my face.

"What do you mean nothing's changed!" I exclaimed. "All this pain for nothing!" I was still only 0.5 centimeters dilated.

We had prayed, confessed Scripture, and believed God for a supernatural childbirth. At that moment I got the revelation that just to get through this thing alive is supernatural!

"Give me drugs!" I yelled. "I want an epidural—like yesterday!" (I'm sure I said please somewhere in there). Just then my mom walked in. I was so relieved to see her. She has an amazing calming presence, and God knew (as did all the nurses) I needed some serious calming.

As the nurse put the epidural in my back and the pain drifted away, I could hear a distant voice, the voice of my mother saying, "Christina, did Mary the mother of Jesus have an epidural?"

No, but it's likely she would have if she was alive in the twenty-first century!

No words can adequately describe what a contraction feels like. However, *extreme, intense,* and *excruciatingly painful* are a few that come to mind. Contractions—the tightening of the muscles in the uterine wall—are the first signs of labor. The baby is on its way! Basically the purpose of a contraction (yes, there is one) is to cause the cervix to dilate (clearly someone forgot to tell my cervix) so the baby can pass through it and out into the world.

Although a lot less graphic (and messy), there is also a period of contraction just before we give birth to our dreams. What we need to understand is that contraction causes the very expansion (stay with me—think uterus) necessary to give birth. Anytime I've moved from one season to the next in my life there's been a time of severe spiritual contraction. This is often accompanied by feelings of incredible containment. It's in this place of contraction and containment that the Holy Spirit does His final work of preparation before catapulting us into the next phase of our destiny. It's also at this time that God is orchestrating and aligning events in order to bring His purposes to pass.

In this season, we may feel like God has forgotten us, that our life is in a holding pattern, or that doors of opportunity have closed. But if we continue to labor by faith, we'll eventually give birth to a healthy dream. It's usually during this intense time of pain that we want to walk away and give up on our dreams. I know this was definitely the case as I was giving birth to our baby. There were several times I tried to escape the labor ward, professing to all within earshot that I didn't want to play anymore!

The strongest and longest contractions in labor take place during the transition phase. This signifies that the whole thing is almost over, and it's also the period men hate most—and they have the fingernail marks to prove it. It takes a singleness of focus to get through this phase, as often it's during the transition from one part of our destiny to another that we experience the most intense testing of our dream.

Too many people abort their dreams at this point of the process because they feel they can no longer stand the contraction and containment. It may cause them to leave their local church, go to another ministry, leave their marriage, or quit Bible college or their job. I believe if people understood the power of containment, far fewer dreams would be aborted or miscarried. It's when we're in a place of containment that God does in us what He needs to, so He can do more through us. The key is not to quit. Don't despise periods of contraction; instead realize it's another vital part of the process.

Be Ready to Adapt

My doctor came in at 8:00 A.M., eager to get to his game of golf. I was still in epidural dreamland. He told me there had been no change in my progress and that he would check on me again after nine holes of golf. He returned a few hours later armed with what looked like a knitting needle. After twelve long hours of being in the hospital, he informed me my water would have to be broken. By now I was acutely aware that nothing was going according to plan. I remember specifically asking God during my daily supernatural childbirth prayer meetings (with Nick) about not having to have my water broken (I never did like knitting).

An hour later and there was still no change. What should have been a simple delivery was now turning into an ordeal, and my doctor was eager to get away on his annual fishing trip with the boys. To try and speed up the process, he added Synctocinon to the drip as this usually speeds up the labor process (another request on my prayer list declined . . . God has a sense of humor).

Surprisingly, in the midst of all the jabs and examinations,

I was totally calm. I was surrounded by the presence of God and I completely trusted Him with my baby (all that praying did work). As the minutes ticked by I noticed a dramatic drop in the baby's heart rate with every contraction. I informed the nurses, and they immediately contacted the doctor. He did a quick checkup and the next thing I heard was, "failure to progress." As they raced me toward the operating room, the nurse explained I would have to have an emergency cesarean section. I couldn't believe it. I had waited seventeen and a half hours for my natural birth—I could have done this two weeks ago!

Things weren't quite like I had envisioned them. I had faith for a completely natural birth. Actually I wanted to be just like my friend Holly who had both of her children at home, in a bathtub, with a midwife. I am sure there is a medical term for that type of childbirth . . . *insanity*! It wasn't until I was actually in labor that I understood I would have my own (not Holly's) birthing experience. The last thing I imagined while praying in my kitchen for a pain-and drug-free delivery was that the baby would get so distressed I would need to have a C-section. As much as I would have loved a conventional delivery, my goal was a healthy baby, and I was going to do whatever was necessary to ensure this was achieved.

Similarly, each of us will give birth to our dreams in our own unique way. The actual process doesn't always go according to our plan. All the skills we learn during the process of carrying our dreams are the things we need to draw on in the critical stage of delivery. We need to remain flexible and be ready to make any necessary adjustments. Our willingness to continually reevaluate our plan, especially when we experience resistance, disappointment or temporary failure, is pivotal. We must accept change and adapt to any difficulties we might face.

Imagine if I had refused to have a C-section because it did not fit into my original plan. You would have thought I was insane for putting my unborn child (and myself) at risk. However, this is exactly what some of us do with our dreams. We end up having a stillborn dream (spiritually speaking) because we're more absorbed with the details of the process than the final outcome. All too often I have seen people who don't get a job offer straight after graduating from Bible college allow the disappointment of this to cause them to walk out on God's plan for their life. Others expected to be married by the age of twenty, but when it didn't happen, they went out and married the first guy they met, settling for less than God's best. Then there are those who were expecting a financial breakthrough, but when it didn't come they stopped tithing. Now they're facing an even bigger financial crisis.

We have to guard against losing sight of our dream when things don't go according to plan by reminding ourselves that God is in control, not us. We must stay flexible and be willing to adjust. We should never get so caught up in the process that we forget the goal.

It's Finally Here

I was supernaturally calm as they prepped me for surgery (perhaps it was the epidural). Nick came into the operating room with me, which was an absolute miracle after our childbirth class experience. Together we prayed that the baby would be fine and that the surgeon would have a steady hand (and that Nick would still be upright at the end of it all). The doctors went to work behind a screen, which at one point moved slightly, giving me a glimpse of the cutting, bleeding, and stretching that was going on. I knew instantly I wasn't called to be a doctor.

Ten minutes later (Nick still standing), there she was— beautiful Catherine Bobbie, in the world at last. Her screams were indicative of the fact that she wanted everyone in the ward to know she had arrived. Our sheer exhaustion was surpassed only by our complete elation. This feeling was better than anything we ever could have imagined. To finally be able to hold our seven-pound, eight-ounce little girl was amazing and surreal.

For nine months her life consisted of floating in a sac of fluid inside of me, and now here she was! She was truly beautiful in every way. Her little hands, her little feet, and her little face were perfectly formed. I couldn't believe the miracle that I was holding. Forty weeks earlier the only evidence of this life was a thin blue line.

It was hard to fathom that she was ours, or that God had entrusted Nick and I with the responsibility of raising this precious life. I realized that our little girl's birth, a dream come true, was only the beginning of a whole new adventure. In that moment all the pain associated with giving birth (or most of it anyway) was forgotten. The whole process was more than worth it.

It's Time to Celebrate

Before I entered the black hole of diaper changings and midnight feedings, I had to take time to celebrate. Family, friends, and flowers began to arrive as the news of Catherine's birth spread. She received so many bouquets and arrangements that the nurses had to place some of them outside in the hallway, and there were enough gifts and outfits to keep her dressed until she was twenty-one!

Nick and I celebrated this amazing occasion with those

closest to us. On day two (three and four) of being in the hospital, it looked like the set of the film *My Big Fat Greek Wedding,* only it was *My Big Fat Greek Baby.* My aunts, uncles, cousins, and second cousins were all there to celebrate with us.

On several occasions the incredible nurses (who were forced to take a Greek sweet every time they left my room) had to enforce a strict numbering system to control our attempt to make it into the *Guinness Book of Records* for the most people squeezed into a hospital room.

When we give birth to our dream we also need to ensure we take time to celebrate our success. For a long time I struggled with celebrating my successes. In the past, when I reached a milestone or experienced a level of accomplishment, I was already focused on the next challenge. I rarely took time to reflect and assess the dream that had just become a reality.

In recent years, some great friends have taught me how to take time to celebrate my achievements before running headlong into the next one. It's so important that we take time to stop, reflect on how far God has brought us, and express our gratitude to Him (and maybe even throw a little confetti!). Only then are we ready to step into the next season of our life—living the dream. (Besides, any excuse for a party!)

Labor

After labor, I had a little time to think about the things that were pivotal in my surviving the delivery room. Here are just a few things I was extremely grateful for.

1. The Medical Team—The Holy Spirit

The nurses and midwife were an amazing comfort to me, particularly when I had absolutely no clue what was going on. They checked on me, instructed me, and comforted me. God has given us a powerful comforter too, the Holy Spirit, to help us through the pain of birthing our dreams.

➤ We don't have to labor alone. The Holy Spirit is just one scream away!

2. Nick and Mom—Personal Support

I never would have made it through without them. They encouraged me, gave me helpful hints (that was mostly Mom), and even fluffed my pillows! Our friends and family can cheer us on during the bearing down phase of labor, while our leaders and mentors can bring their experience and expertise to help us realize our dream.

> ➤ Although we may have to do the physical pushing alone, make sure you have a support team on whom you can rely.

3. Learning to Breathe—Rest

Despite my reticent attitude toward the Lamaze classes predelivery, I was extremely grateful for them during delivery (even if the only thing I remembered was the importance of breathing!). I learned firsthand the necessity of resting, if only briefly, between contractions. In the throes of giving birth to our dreams, we too need to take advantage of the moments of rest that come our way.

> ➤ Find rest in every situation—It will give you the strength you need to make the final push.
> ➤ Actually take your lunch break (rather than working through it) and relax.
> ➤ Take the long way home after a busy day and spend a few extra moments alone.
> ➤ Make a Sabbath day a priority—a day to rejuvenate yourself (even if it's not Sunday).

- Go and sit on a beach and watch the waves without thinking there are 101 other things you could be doing with that time.
- In the midst of it all, do something that you love to do (shopping?).
- Take a long walk with God (exercise may not feel like rest, but it can be!).
- Sleep—you just may need to rest physically to give yourself time to rejuvenate.

Section 9

REALIZE

✺ Diary Entry

The doctor must have removed part of my brain during the C-section because I seem to have amnesia about everything relating to the birth (it was pain-free after all!). It may have something to do with the fact that I have given birth to the single most gorgeous baby ever to be born. Okay, I may be a little biased.

We had planned and prayed for this baby; she was so wanted. I'm so overwhelmed with a love I never thought possible. It's as if a love bomb has exploded in my heart, opening up a part of me that I didn't know existed (and I'm not referring to the C-section). We were inseparable (thanks to the umbilical cord) during the last nine months, and that's exactly how I want it to stay. I can't imagine life without her.

As I have been fulfilling the very last point on my to-do list—lie in hospital bed recovering (actually the next to last item—I've added a back and foot massage to the list)—I've rediscovered my love of counting. First I count all of Catherine's fingers, then I count her toes, then I touch her ears and her nose, then I count her fingers and toes again (just in case I missed something the nine previous times). She's so perfect in every way—even her used diapers send Nick and me into an excited frenzy! But I do have a question in relation to filled diapers . . . how can all that gunk (and all that smell) come out of something so small? It could be bottled and used in chemical warfare!

On the topic of diaper changing, people told me it would come easily as long as I used disposable diapers. I even did a few practice runs during the preparation phase of my pregnancy. All I had to remember was the sticky tabs face the front, and if the diaper slips off once the baby is upright, it's a good sign I've been overcautious about not wanting to suffocate her tummy. What I wasn't expecting was the hospital's total ban on anything disposable. I wish they had warned me; I would have made one-handed safety-pin opening a priority in the training leading up to giving birth. As hard as I try, I can't get the cloth diapers to stay on. The biggest obstacle is getting the pin through four layers of cloth. I have even tried running the pin through my hair, as I've been told the natural oils lubricate the safety pin making it easier to get through the layers. All I've successfully been able to do is prick my scalp with the pin! (Note to self: get Nick to smuggle in some disposable diapers.)

Bath time is hilarious. You need to be a contortionist to make it happen. She's so tiny and fragile that I'm scared I'm going to break her. Yesterday morning was the first time Nick and I had to bathe her on our own (at least that was the intention). He prepared the bath (elbow thermometer at the ready), while my job was undressing Catherine and actually giving her the bath. I ran into a little trouble when I had to open the baby soap while ensuring the baby's head stayed above water. I pretended my stitches were hurting so the nurse would come and help.

Now breastfeeding (I have a newfound compassion for cows), I have enough milk to feed a small nation. The electronic breast pump contraption is insane. Perhaps it's payback for me laughing at the cows that were getting milked during my third grade excursion to a dairy farm. The other thing I didn't realize is that I remain in coffee and chocolate exile as long as I'm breastfeeding! (Note to God: This hardly seems fair.)

I have always leaned toward being obsessive, but being a mom has cemented the tendency. I check on Catherine's breathing at least thirty-five times a day. I can't see her chest going up and down under all the blankets, so I put my face up against her to feel if she's breathing (at least it's not a mirror over her mouth). The nurses must think I'm neurotic! (Note to self: stop obsessive behavior.)

The C-section also means I have a little tummy cut. Although the stitching seriously impedes me doing very much (including walking, laughing, and going to the bathroom), I'm so excited that the incision is so tiny I can still wear a bikini. (Vanity is a funny thing; just forty-two hours ago I didn't care who saw me from what angle, I just wanted the baby out . . . and now I'm concerned about a five centimeter cut!) What am I thinking? Bikinis? My stomach is so bloated, I still look like I'm pregnant. How is it that with the baby, the placenta, and all that other stuff that left my body, I still look like I have to give birth? It's all a cruel joke I say.

The doctor (yes, he made the fishing trip) popped in earlier today and suggested Nick and I have a date night sometime before I'm discharged. This is so we can have some romantic time together before we leave the nurses far, far behind (oh, how I hope I have mastered breastfeeding, diaper changing, and bath time by then). So tonight was date night. Once the nurses assured me that Catherine would be fine without me for two hours (they promised to check on her breathing), the next most pressing matter was what I was going to wear. The only thing I could fit into, other than my maternity clothes, was my pajamas. Nick convinced me that leaving the hospital in my pj's and slippers might not be appropriate, so back to the elastic waistbands I went. (Note to self: from here on out elastic is banished from my wardrobe).

I fed Catherine and put her in the nursery so Nick and I

could have our date. I was stunned by the amazing gift God had given us. Above her crib her little name card brightly displayed her name—Catherine Bobbie. So much thought had gone into choosing her name, and this wasn't just because she would have to live with it forever. Nick and I decided to name her after the two women who have had the most profound impact on my life: my mom, Catherine, and my pastor, Bobbie.

I had to have one last glance at her before I left, and that was all it took. As I looked at Catherine Bobbie sleeping peacefully, so loved and so wanted, I began to sob. I was taken back thirty-five years to a nursery in a hospital on the other side of Sydney. There too a baby girl lay sleeping, but the name card above her crib said Unnamed. *In fact, her mother was preparing to leave her at the hospital, apparently unwanted. That little girl was me.*

More than three decades later, I stood over Catherine's crib, overcome by emotion. I was struck by a powerful realization that in just one generation, Jesus could change everything. A relationship with Jesus unlocked my potential and helped me discover my divine purpose, and now it was impacting the generations through the life of my little girl. It was because of Him that I was staring at a hope and dream realized. My gratitude to God is immeasurable.

As I looked at Catherine, I thought back over the last nine months—the all-day nausea; the sleepless nights; the discomfort; the enlargement and its consequences (maternity wear!); the en-

durance; the preparation; and finally the labor. All of this so I could give birth to my dream (and I'd do it all over again). It's hard to imagine that this precious life lying in the crib started out as little more than a thin blue line. She is both a dream realized and a dream that's just beginning—a life yet to be unleashed.

A Final Note

❦

It's Only Just Begun

As I write this, Catherine and I are debating over why she shouldn't substitute her wading pool or our new carpet for the potty. I'm definitely losing this argument, and I'm more certain than ever that this child is going to become a defense attorney! Nowadays this sequence of events takes place with increasing regularity as do chats about the virtue of peas and vegetables over chocolate and ice cream, and why going down the slide headfirst isn't really appropriate.

Our little girl, Catherine Bobbie (now more widely known as Catie-Bob), has a well-developed will of her own. So much so that she sometimes needs reminding of the roles and responsibilities that go along with the titles "Mom and Dad" and "daughter." It takes all the restraint I have to resist succumbing to Catie's every wish and command, particularly when she looks into my eyes, head lowered, and whispers, "Sorry Mommy." (You think I'm bad, you should see Nick!)

My mom, who often sits smugly watching these hilarious exchanges (she doesn't think most two-year-olds really know the meaning of *boundaries* even if they nod when you're explaining they shouldn't overstep yours), likes to remind me that Catherine's iron will and sheer determination are genetic traits. She thinks maybe now I understand just how much angst I put her through when I was a little girl!

The truth is I wouldn't trade a single moment of motherhood for anything in the world. No, not even the day of Catherine's baby dedication. Imagine it, the Caine family dressed in all their finery excitedly sitting in the front row of church waiting for Catie-Bob's stage debut. As she played with the ribbons on her cute little dress and stared at her brand-new shoes, there was no indication of the events that were about to unfold.

Flooded by complete adoration for my little girl, I took her from her daddy's arms and put her over my shoulder so the nice people sitting behind us could see just how cute our girl's smile was. Right at that moment what seemed to be the torrents of Niagara Falls poured over my new shirt (oh the stench!). What's worse than being used for target practice by one's baby is having to get up to preach wearing the same shirt that was spotless just a few moments before. Let me tell you, it was tough sticking to my notes when the pervading smell was that of baby vomit.

It was ironic that I had spent the first three months of my pregnancy nauseous and sick, and now the cause of my sickness was projectile-vomiting all over me! The irony was lost on me at the time, but later I realized just how full a circle we'd come. The dream Nick and I had conceived and finally birthed was actually just phase one of the adventure.

Back at the rice grain stage of my pregnancy, it was difficult to see beyond the labor ward to Catherine's future. But as soon as she arrived, Nick and I began to dream new, more vivid dreams for our little princess. There were short-term dreams such as having her sleep all the way through the night (lots of prayer went into this one), weaning her off milk and onto solids, seeing her take her first step, and hearing her say her first word (Nick wants the world to know that it was *Daddy*). But we also have longer-term dreams for Catie-Bob. We have dreams for everything from her education and spiritual walk, to the man she will end up marrying (Nick is still in denial about this one).

You see, as one dream is fulfilled another is conceived and the process of believing, envisioning, positioning, enduring, enlarging, preparing, and laboring starts all over again. It's an ongoing cycle. The only way we continue to press on toward the purposes of God for our lives is to keep dreaming. We will never arrive or fulfill our destinies this side of eternity, so like Paul we should be passionate about embracing every new stage of the journey, never assuming we've arrived.

> Not that I have already attained, or am already perfected; but I press on, that I may lay hold of that for which Christ Jesus has also laid hold of me. Brethren, I do not count myself to have apprehended; but one thing I do, forgetting those things which are behind and reaching forward to those things which are ahead, I press toward the goal for the prize of the upward call of God in Christ Jesus. *(Philippians 3:12-14 NKJV)*

There is so much more for us to do and become—bigger mountains to climb; more people to influence; more fears to conquer; lives to be won into the Kingdom; and greater promises to possess. We cannot stop or settle where we are. God wants us to keep pursuing Him and the dreams He has for us. As long as we're alive, God has a purpose for our lives.

It's Generational

I was in England recently preaching at a women's conference in a town located close to Stratford-Upon-Avon, the birthplace of William Shakespeare. Having studied English literature in college, I am an avid Shakespeare fan, so I decided to go on a little tour of the town.

As I wandered through the streets overawed by the town's history and imagining what it might be like to live back in Shakespeare's day (puffy dresses and lots of men in tights), I noticed a shop sign that read, "Discover your roots—family history available inside." Confident that my maiden name, Caryofyllis, wasn't going to appear on the list (and realizing that it wasn't my biological family name anyway), I decided to try the name Caine, as Nick is from good English stock.

Thinking perhaps I had married into royalty I was eager to find out if Nick was the only living ancestor of a long lost uncle of aristocratic blood who had left his entire estate to one Nicholas Caine, Esq. Caught up in how I would decorate our new country manor, I was startled by the woman behind the counter who had completed the Caine genealogy. As I looked at the sheet of paper my bubble was tragically burst at the realization that Nick's ancestors were far from royal. The list was dotted with criminals, convicts, paupers, and pirates!

Although Nick's family tree wasn't everything I hoped it would be, looking at the past gave me a new perspective on the future. As I thought about how colorful Nick's family history was, and the fact that I didn't even know mine, I was struck by how different the lives of our descendants would be. I laughed as I stood on the street that day knowing that because I had chosen to follow Jesus, and Nick had decided to do the same, we were not only altering our lives, but the generations to come. A family history that had once been defined by immorality, poverty, alcoholism, divorce, criminality, adultery, and abuse would now be characterized by faith, love, peace, and joy. Our descendants would one day thank Jesus that Nick and I had given our lives to Him.

We all have the power to leave a legacy. The past doesn't have to limit our future—we have the power to change it. We can fulfill our destiny, we can realize our dreams, and we do have the capacity to impact and influence future generations. God and the world are waiting for your life to be unleashed.

Hold that thought . . .

By the sound of that shriek the end of the world is at hand, or Catie-Bob has pulled the head off her favorite doll again!

It All Starts Here

Thanks for reading *A Life Unleashed*. I hope you're now inspired and challenged to see your own life and dreams unleashed. My heart's desire is that you will fulfill the purpose for which God put you on the planet. To do this, you must first ensure that Jesus Christ is the foundation of your life. Jesus is the source and completer of our dreams and destinies. He said, "I am the Way and the Truth and the Life; no one comes to the Father except by (through) me" (John 14:6). If you have never had a relationship with Jesus, or perhaps you once had but you're away from Him, right now I want to encourage you to pray this prayer:

Dear Jesus,

I'm sorry I've been living my life my own way and ignoring you. Right now I want to make the decision to stop living my life my own way and begin living it your way.

I ask that you would forgive me for all of my sins, give me a brand-new start today and a hope for the future.

I want to be a Christian, a follower of Jesus Christ, for the rest of my life.

Amen

If you have prayed this prayer, congratulations! I would love to hear from you. Please contact me at: chriscaine@ chriscaine.com.

Love,
Chris

Endnotes

꩜

[i] Meyer, Joyce. *Do It Afraid!* New York: Warner Faith, 2003.

[ii] Barnett, Tommy. Sermon given at the Hillsong Conference, Sydney, Australia, July 2000.

[iii] Churchill, Winston. "These Are Great Days: Speech given to the Harrow School in London, England." http://www.weeks-g.dircon.co.uk/quotes_by_author_c.htm.

Thank You

Where do I start? There are just so many family, friends, and associates who helped me give birth to *A Life Unleashed* (and some assisted with birthing Catherine too).

There's my husband, Nick, the most amazing (and ravishing) man on the planet and a constant source of love and support. You are my life partner and you continue to draw out of me all the potential that is not yet seen. I thank God daily that you had hope and faith where others had given up.

Maria (a genius of the highest order), my friend and partner in Christ. You spent countless hours reading, writing, editing, and critiquing this manuscript. We laughed, drank coffee, laughed, drank more coffee, forgot to sleep, and communicated across the world via phone and e-mail to bring this baby home. You now know more about pregnancy (the good, the bad, and the ugly) than any other nonmother I know. This was a combined effort—the book wouldn't be here without you.

Immeasurable gratitude and thanks go to my pastors, Brian and Bobbie Houston, who have allowed me the privilege of serving with them to reach a lost world and build His Church. Without you, I wouldn't be here. (Special thanks also go to Bobbie for stepping in for Nick at the childbirth classes).

I thank Joyce Meyer for believing in me. Your life continues to be a source of inspiration.

Holly, big, big thanks to you for your friendship, love, support, inspiration, and oh-so-many laughs! You have so helped me become who I am today.

Tiffany (nanny extraordinaire), a gift to our family . . . and Catherine will forever be grateful for the pink ribbons and dresses.

My friend Shanelle was there with Maria and I in Copenhagen, sipping coffee, eating chocolate, and singing John Denver hits as we first began planning this book.

To our awesome team: Maree, Ann, Cindz, Lorren, Suzi, Rachel, Alex, Virginia, Wayne, Carol, Kathy, Leah, Nick, Leanne and Flavius Cornelius. They were often quiet (sometimes with a little prompting), carried the extra load, prayed for us, and were a constant source of laughter and inspiration.

Monica (the Canada connection), whose input and insight, particularly in the hotel room at 1:00 A.M. in the morning, was invaluable. You're amazing and I can't thank you enough.

To our new partners at Time Warner (particularly Rolf and Jennifer). Thank you for the incredible opportunity to share this book with others.

Particular thanks goes to Annie, Amanda, Di, Wendy, Daryl-Anne, and Selina who were kind enough to read the manuscript, check grammar, and give their candid feedback (and Maria's mom for keeping her fridge well stocked during her time in the book bubble).

Special, special thanks go to my Dad and Mom for showing me what unconditional love is.

To my biological mother, wherever you are, I thank you

for having the courage to see beyond the thin blue line and for allowing my life to be unleashed.

And to Jesus Christ for the price He paid. It's all because of Him and it's all for Him.

About the Author

Christine Caine is a young, dynamic, and passionate vision-
ary whose powerful testimony of restoration is impacting
thousands of lives around the world each year. She, her husband, Nick, and daughter, Catherine, live in Sydney and are
pastors at Hillsong Church.

Personal experience and her grasp of the issues shaping
the twenty-first century enable her to effectively communicate a relevant message of hope.

As one of Australia's leading communicators, and a Director
of Equip & Empower Ministries, Christine's inspiring message
is influencing the lives of leaders, women, youth, the wider
church, and the unchurched across the world.

Her vision is to help people overcome the obstacles, hur-
dles, and challenges of life and maximize their God-given
potential and purpose.

For more information about other Christine Caine resources or booking information, please visit: www.christine caine.com.

Don't miss *Ending Your Day Right*
by Joyce Meyer

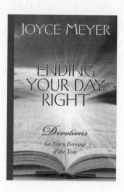

A companion to popular communicator Joyce Meyer's previous devotional, *Starting Your Day Right*, this pocket-sized treasure will help you seek God at the end of your day. It aims to help you take time to acknowledge and give thanks for God's presence throughout your day, and to ask for His continued care throughout the night. Topics include:

- The keys to letting go at the end of the day
- Remembering to count your blessings
- Living secure in God's love
- Realizing your hopes and dreams
- Giving thanks for the things you have.

Allow Joyce to guide you through Scriptures and devotions specifically geared toward ending your day right.

Coming October 2004

Don't miss *Intimate Faith*
by Jan Winebrenner

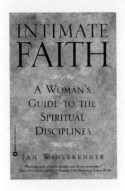

In her engaging manner, gifted communicator Jan
Winebrenner presents seventeen classic spiritual disciplines that enable women to pursue joyful, godly
living and spiritual intimacy with the Almighty.
Intimate Faith introduces these disciplines and provides biblical proofs as well as present-day illustra-
tions to show how God uses them to increase your
capacity for enjoying Him and experiencing the full-
ness of His desires for your life. Specific attention is
given to principles such as: humility, meditation,
fasting, simplicity, sacrifice, celebration, and confes-
sion. Through the cultivation of all seventeen disciplines, you can develop as a disciple of Christ,
learning to nurture a truly unshakable faith.

Jan Winebrenner is the founder of the Dallas
Christian Writers Guild. She has also written articles
for *Today's Christian Woman* and *Decision Magazine*
and is a regular speaker at women's events and con-
ferences.